Visions Beyond the Veil

H.A. Baker

Sovereign World

Sovereign World Ltd
PO Box 777
Tonbridge
Kent TN11 0ZS
England

Originally published by Osterhus Publishing House, Minneapolis, Minnesota, USA.

ISBN 1 85240 278 4

The publishers aim to produce books which will help to extend and build up the Kingdom of God. We do not necessarily agree with every view expressed by the author, or with every interpretation of Scripture expressed. We expect each reader to make his/her judgement in the light of their own understanding of God's Word and in an attitude of Christian love and fellowship.

Typeset by CRB Associates, Reepham, Norfolk.
Printed in England by Clays Ltd, St Ives plc.

Contents

Foreword

I cannot remember a time when I was not aware of the things of God, of angels and demons, of heaven and hell, of judgement and the life to come. I have never been able to imagine a life without Jesus. I never had to be convinced of the supernatural, or that there had to be more to life than could be found here on earth. I was simply introduced to the spiritual world by being born into a Pentecostal missionary family in the town of Kunming, China, where the events of this book took place.

My father and mother were both born in China too. They returned after World War II to found a Bible school in Kunming, where my father had spent his childhood years. He in turn was there because a generation earlier my grandfather had determined to obey the Great Commission and journey to the ends of the earth to tell the Good News of Jesus.

H.A. Baker, as my grandfather was always known, chose the furthest reaches of south-west China as his field of service. He was dedicated, persevering for years with little fruit until he nearly gave up. But the Holy Spirit came into his life with power, he continued on in China, and then he saw with his own eyes one of the most wonderful outpourings of the Holy Spirit recorded in all of Church history.

To me it seemed natural. If the Bible was true, why shouldn't God confirm His Word through such visions, revelations and spiritual gifts? Why shouldn't we experience the reality of God if we seek Him according to Scripture? Why shouldn't the supernatural things of God become increasingly normal as we draw closer to Him?

I heard more of these things on every occasion I spent time with my grandfather. I first remember him in Hong Kong, after we had all been forced to leave China soon after the revolution of 1949. I would sit on his lap, and he would pour his memories into me – new stories every time – of angels and demons, miracles, power encounters, infillings of the Holy Spirit, winning the lost, serving the King. What a normal way to live!

Later we, and many other China missionary families, moved to Taiwan. Of course my grandfather gravitated there to a minority group, learning a new and difficult dialect of Chinese, and continuing his long pattern of reaching lost sheep wherever they could be found. He and my grandmother lived simply, as the Chinese did. He did not appeal for support. He gave away what he did not need. He earned the love and respect of missionaries all over Taiwan, even those whose methods were very different from his. And I could never forget his witness, even for a moment.

My grandfather's ministry represented a blend of Word and Spirit that has carried my faith all these years. He never let miracles and manifestations divert him from the teachings of the Bible, nor did his faithfulness to the Word become a hesitancy to drink in the realities of all that is testified to in that Word. He was careful. He searched the Scriptures to verify what he heard and saw, and he found the living God in those Scriptures. He made sense to me; he shaped my life.

He also intimidated me. For a long time I never thought I could carry on a ministry like his in any way. It was wonderful, but such work was for unusual saints, not ordinary people like me. But over the years my memories of *Visions Beyond the Veil* continued to fuel the hunger for revival in my heart until I could no longer be 'ordinary'.

Living in revival, around the throne of Jesus, thrilled with Him and anything that has to do with Him, has become the only appealing way of life to me.

Now my wife Heidi and I are in Africa, working among the poorest people we can find, taking in orphaned and abandoned children and looking for lost sheep everywhere we can. And Jesus is again revealing Himself to 'the least of these', just as he did in Kunming, China, so many years ago in my grandfather's orphanage. That outpouring was not in vain; it was not just for the benefit of a few isolated people in a faraway country. Its story has fired hearts among the spiritually hungry around the world for two, and now three generations, and it is being continued today in those who will be like children in His sight.

My grandfather saw among his beggar orphans how the Holy Spirit could graciously bring the delights of heaven into even the most miserable hearts. He saw the heart of Jesus, who can and does wipe away every tear from the eyes of those He rescues from the hand of Satan. And if He can transform illiterate, wretched and forgotten orphans in remote China into monuments of His grace, and pillars of His church, then He can redeem us in every way too. He is good, and we will love Him forever!

Rolland E. Baker
Africa, April 2000

Introduction

This book tells the story of a most unusual move of the Holy Spirit that took place at an orphanage in the Yunan Province of China. The Adullam Rescue Mission in Yunnanfu was the home to children, mostly boys ranging in ages from six to eighteen, who had been beggars on the streets in the city, or who were orphans and had been brought to the home when one or both parents died. Some were children who for one reason or another had run away from their homes in more distant parts of this or adjoining provinces. These children were baptized in the Holy Spirit and received extraordinary revelations and visions from God.

When the children arrive at the home, they are uneducated and undisciplined. Before coming to us they had often been part of gangs, surviving by begging and stealing, and had learned to live by the laws of the street.

In the Adullam Home, the children learn about the Bible and hear the gospel. Those coming into the home have always been open to the teachings given and some were doubtless already converted when the Holy Spirit began to move in power, while others had a very good knowledge of the main themes of the Bible.

All those who received the Holy Spirit knew enough about the faith to believe in one God and to understand they could only be saved by the blood of Christ. They prayed to be filled with the Holy Spirit and spent time seeking the Lord. We did not see any one of them specifically seeking any of the visions or manifestations that they received day by day as they waited on Him. Throughout all the weeks of this move of the Spirit they prayed and praised the Lord, and sought to bring glory to His name alone.

The Lord treated all the children impartially. The oldest and the youngest, the first arrivals and the most recent comers, the best and the worst – their heavenly Father blessed them all equally with His wonderful heavenly gifts.

This giving of the Promised Spirit was clearly a love gift of grace which had nothing to do with 'works' or personal merit. It was not something that was worked up. It was something that came down. It was not the result of character building achieved on a human level. It was a blessing of God freely given from above.

No natural explanation

There is no natural explanation for the experiences of these Adullam children, because:

1. These wonders **could not possibly have been the product of the children's natural minds**. Such uneducated, mentally untrained, unimaginative boys as these could not have imagined such things themselves.
2. These spiritual experiences, visions and revelations **could not have been the working of the subconscious mind**. Many of these children were too young, too ignorant, or too recently rescued from their own godless background to know the Bible teaching on these subjects.
3. They **cannot be explained by the psychology of mental suggestion from others**. We ourselves had never seen such visions, never been in meetings where they had occurred, and never even read or heard of visions like the ones that were given to these children. These experiences were new to all of us.

4. They **did not get these things from one another**. When the power of the Lord fell among us many children were filled with the Spirit at the same time. Children in different rooms sometimes had the same vision simultaneously. There was no possibility of comparing with one another.
5. There is no natural explanation for the fact that the content of the visions **was in complete harmony** and had numerous details in common. Even the most simple children, who could easily be confused on cross questioning, whether questioned on their own or in groups, gave as clear and consistent answers to questions covering great numbers of details as could possibly have been given by any eye witness.
6. Neither can these experiences be explained as any sort of mental excitement, religious frenzy, natural emotion, nervous state, nor any sort of self-produced condition. The Holy Spirit came in power upon normal children in a normal state of mind free from all the conditions just mentioned.

The true Church is supernatural

Supernatural visions and revelations are foundation stones upon which the Church was established and upon which it stands. The whole Bible, Old and New Testament, is a **supernatural** revelation from God.

In the Old Testament, God spoke to His people in a number of ways. He revealed His will by directly inspiring the prophets, bypassing their minds. He appeared to men and women and spoke to them in a 'voice' with 'words' as, for example, He did with Moses, speaking to him as one person speaks to another, face to face (Exodus 33:11). God also revealed Himself in dreams, in visions and in various kinds of supernatural revelations. Angels brought messages to men and women and were continually active as God's ambassadors in carrying out His plan of redemption on earth.

The New Testament likewise claims to be a **superhuman** revelation. Paul said of the gospel he preached:

> *'I did not receive it from any man, nor was I taught it; rather, I received it by revelation from Jesus Christ.'*
>
> (Galatians 1:12)

His writings in his epistles were part of this supernatural *'revelation from Jesus Christ'*.

Without the help of the Holy Spirit and without the kind of visions and revelations that were given at Adullam, there would be no Christianity at all. The true Church only continues to exist today because supernatural manifestations just like these were a natural part of its life from its very beginning and indeed were the reason for its vigorous growth. When Herod wanted to destroy the baby Jesus, the wise men were 'warned in a dream' (Matthew 2:12). An angel appeared to Joseph in a dream (Matthew 2:13); a man from Macedonia appeared to Paul in a vision (Acts 16:8–10). When Paul was praying in the temple at Jerusalem he fell into 'a trance' and saw Jesus, who spoke to him, giving him directions for his work (Acts 22:17). Peter also fell into a trance while praying on the roof of the house. He saw a vision and heard the Lord in what seemed to be an audible voice (Acts 10:13–15). Cornelius had a vision of an angel in broad daylight (Acts 10:1–3). The whole book of Revelation, which is a record of visions given in the Spirit through the ministry of angels, was given to John as a supernatural revelation when he was 'in the Spirit'. Paul either died and in an 'out of the body' experience went up to heaven or was caught up to heaven in a vision like our Adullam children and saw Paradise. He had so many of these supernatural revelations that the Lord had to send him a thorn in the flesh to keep him humble (2 Corinthians 12:1–3).

Angels also had a large part in the work of the first Church. The early disciples were directed in their work by the angels and, in this way, were often protected from imminent danger. An angel told Philip to take the road from Jerusalem to Gaza, where he met the Ethiopian eunuch (Acts 8:26–40). An angel appeared to Paul encouraging him and warning him about the future (Acts 27:23–4). It was directly as a result of an angelic vision that Cornelius and his whole household were saved and then baptized (Acts 10:3). When Peter was in prison, an angel rescued him, unchaining him and then instructing him to get dressed, after which he opened the prison doors and the locked city gate before leading him out into the street (Acts 12:7–8).

But more powerful than all these supernatural interventions was the work of the Holy Spirit. He came as the Lord had promised He would when Jesus returned to His Father.

That first Church did not read prayers. Neither did they say prayers. That first Church prayed to God from their heart, and God directly and supernaturally answered. When the disciples were in danger they got together and prayed to God. This was not formal praying; it was not a passionless, carefully worded prayer meeting to impress human ears. Everybody prayed at the same time: everybody cried to God in a loud voice. This was a special prayer meeting to find an answer for one great need.

When God answered, everybody knew it. The Holy Spirit shook the house in which these people were praying, and everyone was 'filled with the Holy Spirit', with a mighty superhuman power. Then they went out with the fire of God in their very hearts in the very face of death.

The early Church had a living God. Through the Holy Spirit Christ lived among them. He worked in them and through them supernaturally through the gifts of the Holy Spirit.

> *'Now to each one the manifestation of the Spirit is given for the common good. To one there is given through the Spirit the message of wisdom, to another the message of knowledge by means of the same Spirit, to another faith by the same Spirit, to another gifts of healing by that one Spirit, to another miraculous powers, to another prophecy,*

> *to another the ability to distinguish between spirits, to another the ability to speak in different kinds of tongues, and to still another the interpretation of tongues.'*
> (1 Corinthians 12:7–10)

This is the promise of the living God. Christ said that if He should go away it would be better for His people, for they would experience His presence closer to them than ever before. He promised:

> *'But I tell you the truth: It is for your good that I am going away. Unless I go away, the Counsellor will not come to you; but if I go, I will send him to you.'* (John 16:7)

> *'...anyone who has faith in me will do what I have been doing.'* (John 14:12)

If ever there was a living God, if ever there were angels, if ever there was a wonder-working Christ, if the Holy Spirit was ever given, if the Bible is a supernatural revelation from God, then we should expect to experience the trances, visions, revelations and working of the Holy Spirit that were given at Adullam. They are normal experiences in the supernaturally founded, supernaturally filled and supernaturally directed Church of the New Testament – the only Church the Bible is interested in.

Chapter 1

The Holy Spirit Comes in Power

The morning prayer meeting was lasting longer than usual. The older children left the room one by one to begin their studies in the school-room, while a few of the smaller boys remained on their knees, deep in prayer. The Lord was near; we all felt the presence of the Holy Spirit among us. Some who had gone out came back into the room.

Tears began to stream down the faces of all those present as they came under a strong conviction of sin – something we had been praying for for a long time – and, with their arms in the air, they cried to the Lord for forgiveness. One person after another fell down under the mighty power of the Holy Spirit until more than twenty were lying flat on the floor. When I saw that the Lord was doing a really unusual thing among us, I slipped over to the school-room and told the boys that if they felt led to come and pray they might be excused from their school work. In a short while the Chinese teacher was left sitting alone by the table. All his pupils had returned to the prayer room, and were now enthusiastically praying and praising the Lord. When the teacher realized there was nothing for him to do, he decided to go home. I had not invited him to come in with the children for, although he had been with us a long time, he did not seem at all interested in spiritual things. He went a short distance from the house but then turned back. When he entered the prayer room no one noticed him; everyone was too busy having their own dealings with the Lord. He went to a far corner of the room, and, for the first time in his life, knelt down and tried to pray.

As there was such a strong sense of the Lord's presence I felt it best to leave the young man by himself and not to intrude on what I knew must be the work of the Spirit and Him alone. It was not long before I noticed the teacher with his arms in the air, tears on his face, pleading with the Lord to forgive his sins, which I heard him say were many. He was a proud man and the fact that he was prepared to humble himself in the presence of his pupils was evidence that the Holy Spirit was really at work.

The meeting went on hour after hour with the children showing no desire to leave. I had nothing to do or say; the Lord seemed in complete control; I just tried to keep out of His way.

As the children saw, in their visions, the awfulness of hell, the despair of those who were lost, and the indescribable evil of the devil and his angels, their agonized crying was beyond anything I had ever experienced before. It was all incredibly real to them. In their visions many saw themselves in chains being dragged to the very edge of hell, which became an awful and terrible reality. As they realized they were sinners in the grip of the devil, who ought to be punished, they were terrified. But the grace of the Lord Jesus to bring freedom was just as real. The joy, laughter and peace they received and the knowledge of what they had been saved from was an experience which I am sure will never leave them.

Since they had all been in the presence of the Lord from early that morning, by the time their late afternoon meal was ready I thought surely the service would be over for the day. That was not the case. Some left the prayer room for a short while but they soon all came back saying that they wanted to wait on the Lord all night. We had never experienced anything like this before – up until that time an hour-long service had been too long for some of them. We had always wanted them to pray more: now that they actually wanted to, why refuse them? None of the children went to bed until very late that night, and it wasn't until 6.00 am the next morning that the last voices finally became quiet. The prayer and praise service that had lasted over twenty hours with hardly a pause finally came to an end.

Josephine Baker

The outpouring continues

After the first two days there was not such a strong sense of God's presence as there had been and we went back to our normal routine, expecting to spend more time waiting on the Lord in the evening. The boys occupied themselves with their school-work and I went out to call on some people and speak to them about the gospel.

Our morning prayer meeting began at about half-past-seven each day. That morning as usual we all prayed at the same time, and each person left when they wanted to. When I returned at twelve o'clock I heard someone praying in the prayer room. Going in to see who it was, I found our quietest and most timid boy, Wang Gi Swen, a boy of about eight years of age, hidden behind the organ praying in a loud voice and weeping as he confessed his sins to the Lord. He had been praying continuously since the morning service without stopping for breakfast.

As I came out of the prayer room it was time for the boys to finish their lessons. Normally they would then to go to the garden or to other kinds of industrial work for the rest of the day, but some of them wanted to know if they could stay to pray. Having told them that any who wanted to could stay and pray, a few went to work, while all the others went into the prayer room and began praying. Almost at once there was another outpouring of the Holy Spirit. From that time on the outpouring was continuous and for over a week no more attempts were made to do regular work. We only did what was necessary. Every one spent the rest of the time taking in the great blessings from God.

In the first few days no one paid much attention to eating or sleeping. Whenever the young people began to pray the power of God would come, causing many to fall to the floor. It was impossible to have meals at regular hours without interfering with the work of the Holy Spirit. As the power of God lifted from them, various ones would go out for a time to rest or eat something, and then they would return to the prayer room soon to be under the power of the Holy Spirit again.

These manifestations of the Spirit were so continuous that nearly all day until late in the night some were under His power.

When things became quieter at nine or ten in the evenings we would suggest that they all go to bed and rest until the next morning. Usually several would want to pray and wait on the Lord longer. As these continued in prayer nearly all who had gone to bed would get up and return to pray. During these nights there was not much sleeping. Some of the boys never left the prayer rooms all night. They did not want to sleep. When they felt tired they rested on the floor for a while and then got up to seek the Lord again. Soon they were lost once more in the things of God.

One thing is certain. All that was demanded of us missionaries during this move of the Holy Spirit was that we keep out of the way and did not interfere with His wonderful work. Our part was to open up our own hearts so that we too might have a deeper experience of the heavenly blessings that were being showered upon us.

Our presence or absence in the meetings made little difference. On one of the first mornings we were delayed in getting downstairs. Without being called, one after another of the children had gone into the prayer rooms and begun praying and praising the Lord. After the many interruptions, when we were at last able to get to the prayer rooms, we found several of the younger children lying flat on the floor under the power of the Holy Spirit and singing in other tongues.

From the very beginning our experience of the Holy Spirit at this time – the manifestations, the visions and revelations – was so beyond our own experience and knowledge that my wife and I said to one another that the only resource we had was to believe that God was bigger than the devil. We trusted in God's promise:

> *'Which of you fathers, if your son asks for a fish, will give him a snake instead? Or if he asks for an egg, will give him a scorpion? If you then, though you are evil, know how to give good gifts to your children, how much more will your Father in heaven give the Holy Spirit to those who ask him!'*
> (Matthew 11:11–13)

In all the weeks that followed God proved to us that this promise is true. It set us free from anxiety as we saw and heard the wonderful things of God that took place among us. Every day was different. One wonder followed another, as our wonder-working God took His Adullam refugees from stage to stage and from glory to glory in His school of the Holy Spirit.

Chapter 2

A Supernatural God

The children who had these amazing experiences of the Holy Spirit knew very little of the Bible's teaching on the subject and this confirmed the supernatural nature of their visions. It also proved to us that the New Testament record of the Holy Spirit's activity was really true.

Some children who had never heard us refer to this move of the Holy Spirit as 'the latter rain' actually experienced His presence as rain.

Rain from heaven

As we all prayed and praised the Lord together with closed eyes some of the children seemed to feel drops of water falling on their heads like rain. They were so busy seeking the Lord that they did not want to stop the flow of the blessing by opening their eyes to look around. At the same time, they wondered how it could be raining on them when there was a roof over their heads. But as the raindrops fell on them they felt refreshed. The drops of water seemed to increase until they became a shower and it all seemed so wonderful that they stopped wondering how it could be happening. The drops became a shower, the shower became a great downpour, and the downpour became a deluge filling the room. Eventually they felt as if they were submerged in a wonderful life-giving flood from heaven.

At various different times several children had this same sensation of rain pouring down on them. Six months after the move of the Holy Spirit, and after a 'dry spell', the floodgates of heaven were opened again, and there was another period of the Holy Spirit's blessing. Again two of the small children experienced rain falling on their heads, seeming to penetrate and flood their whole beings.

Through Bible study and through direct revelation by the Holy Spirit, Adullam is now coming to understand the meaning of this 'rain'. We understand that this is what the prophet Joel spoke of:

> *'He has given you the former rain faithfully,*
> *And He will cause the rain to come down for you –*
> *The former rain,*
> *And the latter rain in the first month.'* (Joel 2:23, NKJV)

The 'former rain' fell on the first Church on the Day of Pentecost and in the succeeding two or three hundred years. This is the autumn rain which waters the seed lying dormant in the ground. But then came the winter of the dark ages, when people fell away from God and the Church seemed dead. During that time there came various periods of the Holy Spirit's activity through great revival figures like Luther, Wesley, Fox, Finney, Moody and other servants of God when God's people learned again the principles of salvation by faith and holy living. But now the sprinkling of the Holy Spirit is becoming a shower. The Lord is again casting out demons, healing the sick, raising the dead, and proving Himself the Almighty God to those who believe Him, enabling them to speak with other languages and prophesy by the power of the Holy Spirit.

The harvest is near. There was a limit to 'the former rain' but 'the latter rain' will come in showers to perfect the Church. In that day there will be deluges of rain, the latter rain of the Holy Spirit. The greatest revival the world has ever seen, bringing the greatest miracles, is just ahead. The most wonderful wonder-working Church the world has ever seen is near. According to His promise the Lord will soon pour out His 'Spirit upon all people'.

> *'And afterwards,*
> *I will pour out my Spirit on all people.*
> *Your sons and daughters will prophesy,*
> *your old men will dream dreams,*
> *your young men will see visions.*
> *Even on my servants, both men and women,*
> *I will pour out my Spirit in those days.'*
> (Joel 2: 28–9; see also Acts 2:17–21)

As a result of this final and greatest outpouring of the Holy Spirit God promises:

> *'I will repay you for the years the locusts have eaten –*
> *the great locust and the young locust,*
> *the other locusts and the locust swarm –*
> *my great army that I sent among you.'* (Joel 2:25)

The fruit and the gifts of the Holy Spirit will be restored to the Church. Many will be converted by this Church with its supernatural life and its supernatural ministry.

If you read Acts 2 you will see that this outpouring of the Holy Spirit upon all people is for today. We at Adullam, at any rate, are convinced of this. Many times the Lord has stood among us, made the same promises He made to the first believers, and commissioned us to carry the same gospel in the same power with which He sent out the first disciples. We know that this latter rain is like the former rain, but it is the latter rain that will usher in the Lord's return.

Manifestations of the Holy Spirit

The Holy Spirit has revealed Himself on different occasions and to different people in several ways.

- **As tongues of fire** visible on the head of each person in the room.
- **As wind**, blowing upon them bringing peace and power. Sometimes these breezes were so intense that we have no difficulty in believing the description of the Holy Spirit coming upon the disciples on the Day of Pentecost:

  'Suddenly a sound like the blowing of a violent wind came from heaven and filled the whole house where they were sitting.' (Acts 2:2)

- **As seven lamps**. At times of special outpouring seven lamps of fire were seen being let down from heaven into the middle of the room. At other times, in visions, children saw:

  'Before the throne, seven lamps were blazing. These are the seven spirits of God.' (Revelation 4:5)

  The seven lamps were a picture of the Holy Spirit's presence among us.

In the first days of the move of the Spirit one small boy spoke in pure prophecy as if he were in heaven at the feet of Jesus. The Lord spoke through him in the first person clearing up many things the children did not understand and telling them how to wait on the Lord and to seek the Spirit. At that time the Lord said, 'When the Spirit is among you, do not open your eyes, for that will make it more difficult for you; the Holy Spirit will give you power to preach the gospel, to cast out demons, and to heal the sick. The Holy Spirit is in seven colours, red, blue and other colours.' One of the older boys then said that when the Spirit had been on him he too had seen different colours. Of course I know light is made up of seven colours but I had never thought of the seven lamps before the throne of God, the Holy Spirit, as seven colours. All light comes from God, and God is light.

This manifestation of the Holy Spirit as a great light has been very common. Some children, having opened their eyes to see if it had something to do with the electric light in the room, could scarcely make out the lights because of the overwhelming glory of the light of heaven which seemed to fill the place. These children know what Paul meant when he said that on the Damascus road the light that shone about him was *'a light from heaven'* that was *'brighter than the sun'* (Acts 26:13). After their visions of heaven and this great light brighter and clearer than any they had seen on earth Adullam people know why in the New Jerusalem in heaven

> *'There will be no more night. They will not need the light of a lamp or the light of the sun, for the Lord God will give them light.'* (Revelation 22:5)

> *'...for the glory of God gives it light, and the Lamb is its lamp.'* (Revelation 21:23)

Chapter 3

True to Scripture

At Adullam we experienced many of the results that the Bible promises will follow when the Holy Spirit comes in power. This confirmed to us that what was happening was from God. We would like to mention some of these results.

They knew they were saved[1]

Through their visions and the other ways in which the Holy Spirit impacted their lives the children became deeply aware of their own sinfulness. They realized that there was no hope unless God was merciful to them and helped them. But in their despair God in His grace brought home to them just as clearly the amazing truth that they had been saved. One person after another came to the place where they could say 'I know I am saved.' The Adullam family was transformed as one boy after another met God. The whole atmosphere of the place was changed. There was so much joy and glory that it bubbled over. While the boys were at work preparing ground for a new garden they praised the Lord so much that some of the local lads mocked them with 'Praise the Lord' whenever they met them. When one boy went into a store to buy some nails, before he realized it he said, 'Hallelujah! I want some nails.' This particular tribes boy was one of the first to be filled with the Holy Spirit. One day on his way to work he was so full of joy that he danced down the street praising the Lord.

They spoke in other tongues [2]

Knowing that their sins had been forgiven and that they were born again the children began seeking the Lord more and more. They were carried deeper and deeper into the things of God and, although most of them had no experience of any of the gifts of the Holy Spirit, God had told them to seek Him for His Holy Spirit, and this they did. They were fully immersed, or baptized, in the supernatural Spirit as the apostles and first disciples had been and over twenty of the people at Adullam spoke in other tongues as they did on the Day of Pentecost.[3]

They prophesied [4]

Early on in this move of the Holy Spirit God spoke to us through one of the smallest and humblest of the children. No one present at the time doubted that the Lord was speaking to us directly through that young boy. There was something about the voice, the penetrating power of the words, which gripped our hearts in a way that we can't describe. We had never experienced anything like it before. We all knew we were hearing directly from the Lord. Later, quite a number of the people at Adullam began to prophesy, and we became more and more amazed at the wonderful things that God was doing among us, using those the world despises to reveal His plans and purposes.

They saw visions of unseen worlds [5]

One of the most striking evidences of the work of the Holy Spirit was the way in which He fulfilled this promise:

> *'But when he, the Spirit of truth, comes, he will guide you into all truth. He will not speak on his own; he will speak only what he hears, and he will tell you what is yet to come.'* (John 16:13–14)

The Holy Spirit gave these simple believers, who had only been taught the Bible for a few months, the most amazing revelations of the truths of Christ, His salvation and the future. It was truly wonderful.

The visions were often given to several people at the same time and nearly all them were seen by quite a number. Even some of the very young boys, six years of age, received them. The visions came while they were under the power of the Holy Spirit but it was not like a dream, it was very real. In many cases afterwards the children came to ask if the Bible said anything about certain aspects of what they had witnessed in the visions.

These were some of the visions they saw: Christ tied to a post and scourged; Christ bleeding on the cross while people looked on and scoffed; the body of Christ taken from the cross, carried to the tomb and placed in it, then the tomb being closed; an angel opening the tomb and Christ's resurrection; His appearance to the women, to the disciples by the sea, and to those in the upper room; the ascension of Christ and the descent of the two angels; heaven; detailed visions inside the New Jerusalem in heaven; angels; the redeemed; hell; the condition of the lost in hell; demons; the devil; the great tribulation and what will happen to those who love God and to the beast during that time; the battle of Armageddon; the binding and imprisonment of Satan in the pit; the great supper of God and birds eating the flesh of the kings and world leaders; the coming of Christ with His angels; the sun and moon changed; heaven quake and earthquake and the destruction that will accompany the coming of Christ; the resurrection of those who know God; the marriage supper of the Lamb in Paradise; detailed views of our mansions in heaven and other heavenly scenes.

They studied the Bible

The Holy Spirit created such a great interest in the children, even the smaller ones, in Bible study that they wanted to know if they could stop studying 'earthly books' and just study the Bible.

They prayed and praised God

Since the unseen world had become so real to them, it is no wonder that there was a change in the community's life of prayer and praise. While not everyone spoke in tongues, all except a very few were so filled and anointed with the Holy Spirit that our joyful praise and worship of Christ the King often seemed almost to touch heaven. Although there were times when we wondered if these heavenly citizens would ever come down to earth again, we needn't have worried. The Holy Spirit was clearly very much concerned about those on earth for in one particular prayer meeting boy after boy pleaded with God in real intercessory prayer for the lost, praying that God would use us all as courageous warriors for Him in this battle for righteousness. Their experience of the Holy Spirit made prayer more than a formality for we were all now convinced that our real enemies are the spiritual hosts of wickedness in the heavenly places.

They preached in the power of the Holy Spirit

After two or three weeks of the Lord's dealings with them, nearly all the children wanted to preach the gospel, even the younger ones. When we went out onto the streets we experienced the power and presence of the Holy Spirit. Some of both the younger and older boys hardly seemed like our boys when they preached under the anointing of the Holy Spirit, not timidly and apologetically as before, but with real authority. Hell and heaven, the devil and his power, Christ, His blood and His salvation, were no myths to these boys. They knew the Lord had told them to preach, and they were given the message, *'Repent, for the Kingdom of heaven is at hand.'* We rejoiced as we listened to them preaching with such conviction, warning people to escape from God's anger and explaining salvation in Christ. On some occasions the power of God was especially evident and there was some unusually miraculous preaching.

At the Chinese New Year, when the streets were filled with all sorts of people out for a holiday, having given out thousands of tracts, we formed a circle on the street to preach the gospel. One of the older boys had prepared a sermon on a New Year theme, but when the preaching began, the Holy Spirit came in such power that he suddenly began speaking in another tongue, while someone else interpreted. As soon as the Lord was through with one interpreter that boy would step back and another would feel the anointing to preach. As soon as this person stepped into the circle he would get the interpretation. This went on for an hour or two while as many people listened as could get near enough to hear. People who would never normally listen to the gospel now listened most attentively as these boys spoke with a passion that must have appeared strange and unusual. As we came away from that service conducted by the Holy Spirit in such order and beauty, each preacher having been chosen by the Lord, each one speaking under direct inspiration from Him, we were deeply struck by these wonders from God. This must have been what the preaching of the Church was like in the beginning and what it seemed so clear that the Lord wanted it to be in the end.

Not that speaking in other languages with interpretation was either in the beginning or subsequently to be the **regular** order of preaching, but as 1 Corinthians 14 clearly shows, it is intended to be part of the Lord's method of preaching the gospel in the power and demonstration of the Holy Spirit. In such preaching the mind of the speaker is not engaged: before he opens his mouth he does not know what words the Spirit will speak through his lips. This is pure prophetic preaching.

There were a few other instances of preaching with tongues and interpretation in some of the villages.

The Lord was the preacher on several occasions in our little street chapel. For two or three nights the youthful preachers, under the real anointing of the Holy Spirit, preached the most inspiring sermons I have ever heard from Chinese evangelists. It seemed as if those sermons would stir anyone to repentance.

God showed His love in still greater power a few nights later when a boy in his teens was preaching very powerfully; his eyes suddenly closed and he began to prophesy like an Old Testament prophet under the direct inspiration of the Holy Spirit. His manner suddenly changed; the form of the Chinese sentences became rhythmic and perfect; the address changed to the first person with sentences such as, 'I am the Lord God Almighty, the one true God, who made all things, who now speaks to you through this boy.' 'Against me have you sinned.' I cannot describe the impact of the boy's penetrating words and the sense of having been ushered into the presence of God. The seats of our little chapel were soon filled, while as many people as could see gathered around the door, listening in awe and wonder. If there was the least commotion, the Lord commanded order, speaking through the boy and saying, 'Make no mistake in this matter. Listen carefully and understand. I the Lord God have all authority in heaven and on earth. To me every man and every demon must give account. I know all about every one of you. I know all your sins. I know how many hairs there are on your head. There are fifty-six of you living in sin here tonight. Repent tonight and I will forgive you.' For half an hour or more we were truly in the presence of a prophet, as the Lord in this way rebuked those people for idolatry, ungodliness and all their vices, bringing them to the brink of despair. Then, as in the case of the Old Testament prophets, God spoke of the glories He had prepared for His people. Like a loving father he pleaded with them to repent that night. He spoke of the distress and destruction that would come to their nation in the day of

God's anger. All these things were repeated several times with exhortations to listen to every word as from a God who would hold every person present accountable for his own soul after that night.

When the prophecy was finished the boy sat down. There was not a movement or a whisper. It seemed to me that every person must know that God was speaking. Nearly all those present had come in while the boy's eyes were shut. When the Lord spoke of fifty-six present under the power of the devil and sin, one of the boys carefully counted the people present who did not belong to the Adullam community. There were fifty-six.

Two demons are cast out[6]

The Lord had told the boys through prophecy and direct revelation, 'Demons must obey me.' They saw the Lord prove His word when two demons were cast out of a man.

There is not sufficient space to give full details of the man's history but we had known him for a number of years and he also lived with us for six months. For many years he had been the victim of depression. Because the darkness surrounding his life had been so intense he was ready to take his own life and we had kept him with us to prevent this. He was always sad. Every effort we made to lead him to Christ was completely useless: his mind was completely blind.

The Lord used three people to cast out the demons. One demon, the size of a man, had an awful, black appearance. Several children saw him come out. As the Lord used one boy, suddenly filled with the Holy Spirit for the task, to rebuke the demons, they put up a final fight to keep the man in their possession. The man's hands clenched together, his eyes were shut tight and his whole body became rigid and resisting. Finally the Holy Spirit brought revelation to the man's heart, his body relaxed and his hands went up in praise to God.

Several children saw the demon after he came out, rushing about in great anger and seeking someone to enter or overcome.[7] All the children, having heard the commotion when they were about to eat their meal and come in to see what was going on, were standing about with their hands in the air, thanking and praising God. Since they were all looking to Jesus and were covered by His blood the demon had no chance to get hold of any of them. The schoolteacher, who was not truly converted, also came in and was looking on in curiosity but was not praying. The angry demon, seeing his opportunity, seized this man and threw him to the floor with a thud. The second demon sat on him, preventing him from getting up. Several children saw this. Our gardener, who some years before had been miraculously delivered from opium, saw it too. He was suddenly filled with the Holy Spirit and cast the demon out of the room.

I only saw the two men, the one set free and the other suddenly fall to the floor beside him. I supposed the schoolteacher had fallen to the floor under the power of the Holy Spirit as there was such a strong sense of His presence in the room. When he was able to get up I asked him why he had been crying and why he fell. He said, 'I wept from sheer terror. Something awful happened. Everything became black; I saw myself about to go into a black pit at the foot of a terrible mountain.' While he was on the floor he saw himself being put in chains by the demon and about to be carried off into utter darkness – but he was set free again.

The physical appearance of the man from whom the demons had been cast out changed at once. He spoke of the peace and joy that he now experienced. At the time he was delivered from the demons he was given a vision of heaven. When he lay in bed at night thinking about the Lord he was so happy that he wondered if it was right for him to have such great joy.

Notes

1. *'We know that we live in him and he in us, because he has given us of his Spirit'* (1 John 1:13).
2. *'And these signs will accompany those who believe: In my name they will drive out demons; they will speak in new tongues'* (Mark 16:17).
3. The New Testament contains many other examples of people speaking in tongues. For example, when the Holy Spirit was poured out at the house of Cornelius: *'While Peter was still speaking these words, the Holy Spirit came on all who heard the message. The circumcised believers who had come with Peter were astonished that the gift of the Holy Spirit had been poured out even on the Gentiles. For they heard them speaking in tongues and praising God'* (Acts 10:44–6); when they received the fullness of the Spirit at Ephesus: *'When Paul placed his hands on them, the Holy Spirit came on them, and they spoke in tongues and prophesied'* (Acts 19:6); as Paul did: *'I thank God that I speak in tongues more than all of you'* (1 Corinthians 14:18).
4. *'In the last days, God says, I will pour out my Spirit on all people. Your sons and daughters will prophesy'* (Acts 2:17); *'When Paul placed his hands on them, the Holy Sprit came on them, and they spoke in tongues and prophesied'* (Acts 19:6).
5. *'But when he, the Spirit of truth, comes, he will guide you into all truth. He will not speak on his own; he will speak only what he hears, and he will tell you what is to come. He will bring glory to me by taking from what is mine and making it known to you'* (John 16:13–14); *'In the last days, God says, I will pour out my Spirit on all people . . . your young men will see visions'* (Acts 2:17).
6. *'And these signs will accompany those who believe: In my name they will drive out demons; they will speak in new tongues'* (Mark 16:17).
7. See the story of the boy possessed by an evil spirit in Mark 9:17–27.

Chapter 4

Visions of Heaven

The Bible tells us that the future home of the people of God is 'the third heaven'.[1] It is an actual place, and in this place there is a city, the New Jerusalem. The New Jerusalem is not a figure of speech, a concept expressed in a way people can understand: the Bible tells us it is a real city with a real foundation which God Himself laid.

The book of Revelation describes the New Jerusalem in this way:

> *'And he* [one of the seven angels] *carried me away in the Spirit to a mountain great and high, and showed me the Holy City, Jerusalem, coming down out of heaven from God. It shone with the glory of God, and its brilliance was like that of a very precious jewel, like a jasper, clear as crystal. It had a great, high wall with twelve gates, and with twelve angels at the gates. On the gates were written the names of the twelve tribes of Israel. ... The city was laid out like a square, as long as it was wide. He measured the city with the rod and found it to be 12,000 stadia in length, and as wide and high as it is long. He measured its walls and it was 144 cubits thick, by man's measurement, which the angel was using. The wall was made of jasper, and the city of pure gold, as pure as glass. The foundations of the city walls were decorated with every kind of precious*

> *stone. The first foundation was jasper, the second sapphire, the third chalcedony, the fourth emerald, the firth sardonyx, the sixth carnelian, the seventh chrysolite, the eighth beryl, the ninth topaz, the tenth chrysoprase, the eleventh jacinth, and the twelfth amethyst. The twelve gates were twelve pearls, each gate made of a single pearl. The great street of the city was of pure gold like transparent glass.'*
>
> (Revelation 21:10–12, 15–21)

Those who have been saved live in this great city, which is the home of the angels. It is the location of Paradise, and of the throne of the living God.

Why shouldn't the New Jerusalem be a real city with streets of real gold, with jasper walls and with foundations of precious jewels? Did God so exhaust His resources when He made the universe that by the time He came to heaven He had no gold left? No, here on earth we find a streak of gold or a precious jewel hidden in the rock or in the earth. They are a shadow of true reality. True reality is to be found in the city whose builder and maker is God. The Bible tells us: *'the creation was subjected to frustration . . .'* (Romans 8:20). The gold we cherish, the jewels we love, the cities and great houses we build are only copies of the city which will one day come down from heaven.

In some of the visions they experienced the Adullam children were caught up into the city of God. How they could see the city I do not know. How Paul could be caught up to Paradise, either in the body or out of the body, I do not know. It is outside the natural order of things. At present we do not need to know how. We just need to know the facts. John was shown the city and he was told by the Lord to write down what he had seen and to send it to the churches.

In heaven

In the Spirit, time after time, the Adullam children were caught up into this city – it was not a dream, but a reality.

Their visits were so real to them, in fact, that they supposed their souls had actually left their bodies to go to heaven, or that in some unaccountable way they had gone there, body and soul, just as in daily life they might visit a distant place. Frequently when they were in Paradise and were enjoying some of the heavenly fruit that grew there, they picked some extra to tuck in their clothes to bring back to earth for 'Muh Si and Si Mu' (Pastor and Mrs Baker).

They knew they were only on a visit to heaven and would soon return. Upon returning, when the Spirit lifted from them, they proceeded at once to search their clothes for the delicious fruit they had brought back for us. When they could not find it, a look of great surprise, confusion and disappointment would come over their faces. They could not believe they had not bodily gone to heaven and come back with the fruit in their clothes.

Walking on the streets of the New Jerusalem was just as real to them as walking on the streets of a Chinese city. One day, when walking down the street in bright sunshine, I asked the boys if the visions were as real and as clear as what we saw then. 'Just as real,' they said, 'but much clearer due to the light in heaven, and the white clothes and the fact that it was so clean everywhere, which made it all so much brighter.'

When they were in the Spirit, the children were usually lost to their natural surroundings. In many cases, although they thought they were in heaven, they talked out loud, describing what they could see, and carrying on a conversation that we could all hear. Often they acted out before our eyes what they were doing there.

The Adullam children said they went to the third heaven. As they passed through the first heaven they felt air on their faces. Having passed the second heaven, they looked back on the wonderful beauty of the stars, in much the same way as a person standing on a mountain might gaze down on a the beautiful lights of a city far away in the distance. From this starry heaven they passed on into the third heaven until they came to the heavenly Jerusalem.

As they approached the heavenly city they saw its light in the distance. Coming nearer, they saw the beautiful city wall glowing with its wonderful jasper-coloured light. The foundations were too beautiful to describe, sparkling with red, yellow, orange, purple, blue, green, violet, and all the other colours of the twelve most stunning jewels.

The children described the city in the sky as three cities in one: one suspended above another, with the largest at the bottom and the smallest at the top, forming a pyramid. Since the city John saw is surrounded by a wall and 1500 miles high, Bible scholars have supposed that it is not a cube but a **pyramid**. Of course, our children knew nothing of this, nor had I ever thought of the New Jerusalem as three cities, one suspended above another. God who suspends the worlds in space is well able to suspend these cities in space. The Bible does not give us any details about the internal order of the city.[2]

On one occasion one of our small boys gave a prophecy which I will describe in more detail in chapter 9. In his vision he was at the feet of the Lord. The Lord told him in this prophecy that He had made heaven big enough for everybody, that there were three cities one above another, and that at present His throne is in the upper city.

Since time and distance are nothing in the heavenly realm, there is nothing impossible in such an arrangement. There are three heavens. There were three storeys in the ark, where God kept a remnant of His creation safe. God is three in one. Why shouldn't the city of the Great King have three parts?

Into the heavenly city

The children entered through the pearly gates into the city with its golden streets. Angels in white guarded the gates and welcomed those who entered. And what a reception it was! As the Saviour had promised, those who had been rejected and treated as outcasts in the world were welcomed as kings by these angelic beings.

Through the gates into the city! Angels, angels everywhere. Angels talking, singing, rejoicing, playing harps and blowing trumpets, dancing and praising the King. It was an incredible sight, beyond human imagination. The children were filled with joy – an indescribable joy they had only ever experienced when filled with the Holy Sprit, the heavenly life of God, the 'down-payment of heaven'.

The children clapped their hands with delight; they shouted for joy. Sometimes they rolled on the floor in laughter, and jumped and danced in great delight. Their faces were so transformed by this heavenly joy that its glory seemed to shine on us too. There was no sorrow in this city: no mournful, long-faced religion there, no solemn, morbid hymns. This was a city full of joy, 'joy in the Holy Spirit'.[3]

Thousands and thousands of angels

Once inside the city the children discovered the meaning of the scripture:

> *'But you have come to Mount Zion, to the heavenly Jerusalem, the city of the living God. You have come to thousands upon thousands of angels in joyful assembly . . . '*
> (Romans 12:22)

These happy angels were not only at the gates, they were everywhere. They were always ready to escort the children wherever they wanted to go. They walked with them and talked with them, explaining to them the meaning of things they did not understand, just as they had talked with the apostle John and revealed to him the mysteries of God. Often in these experiences with the angels our children were given harps and taught to play them and sing as the angels did. They were also taught how to blow the trumpets, as well as much more about the music and language of heaven.

The music and language of heaven

When we saw the children, with closed eyes, all dancing around the room in rhythm, we discovered that in their vision they were dancing with the angels in heaven and keeping time with the heavenly music. When we saw them apparently blowing a trumpet or going through the motions of playing a harp, we found that in the vision they were joining the heavenly orchestra praising the King. We could not see the heavenly harps or trumpets; we could not see the angels' joyful dance or hear their song; we could only hear the children singing heavenly songs. It was a daily occurrence to find a child, lying comfortably on some pine needles in a corner on his own, going through the motions of playing a harp. Going up to him, we could hear him singing a new song we had never taught him. As we got nearer still, we would discover that the words were as strange to us as the tune. The singer was singing in the heavenly choir. His song was the song the angels taught him. The words of the song must have been in the language of angels. Seeing the children singing in this heavenly angelic choir was unforgettable. Sometimes several of them in some place in the heavenly city or its wonderful Paradise would decide to play and sing together. With closed eyes, while completely under the power of the Holy Spirit, three or four of them would go off by themselves. If we were nearby we would hear them consult about who would play the trumpet and who would sing. After all was decided and everybody was ready, the heavenly songs began. The trumpeters held their hands up in front of them and blew as if they were blowing trumpets. The harpists both played and sang, while those without instruments joined in the singing. In these cases they always sang in languages we did not understand, unless by mutual agreement they decided to sing one of those hymns they 'used to sing down on earth'. In that case they sang in Chinese.

Seeing and worshipping Jesus

The climax of all the heavenly joy and wonder was 'seeing Jesus' and worshipping the One who had saved them by His blood.

Soon after entering the gates of the city the children were taken by the angels to 'go and see Jesus'. We could hear them talking about 'going to see Jesus' and watched as in the vision they approached the throne of Christ. When they came into His wonderful presence they stood reverently gazing with love and devotion at the Lord of all creation, who was also their Saviour. First of all they thanked Him, and then clasping their hands in front of them they bowed low before Him in respect and loving adoration. Then they knelt and bowed their faces to the floor in true worship 'in spirit and in truth', in a way that few on earth know unless they have experienced the baptism of God's Holy Spirit.[4]

The throne of God and the throne of Christ

The children, like the apostle John, saw the throne of Christ:

> *'...there before me was a throne in heaven with someone sitting on it. And the one who sat there had the appearance of jasper and carnelian. A rainbow, resembling an emerald, encircled the throne. Surrounding the throne were twenty-four other thrones, and seated on them were twenty-four elders. ... Before the throne seven lamps were blazing. These are the seven spirits of God.'*
>
> (Revelation 4:3–4, 5b)

Jesus is pre-eminent

No matter how amazed the children were by all the wonderful things they saw in the golden city, no matter how happy they were in all the fun of Paradise, no matter how full of joy in the presence of the angels, Jesus was never forgotten. His name was mentioned in every conversation; His praise was mingled in with every enjoyment; He was praised everywhere, in everything, and by everybody.

A house for everyone

On either side of the beautiful golden streets were buildings side by side, with rooms opening onto the street. There was a room for every single person in heaven. Set into the door and the front of the house were precious jewels which shone so brightly that the building radiated with light and glory. The name of each occupant was written above the door. The angels took the children to their room. In all the rooms there were the same kinds of furnishings: a beautiful golden table upon which there was a Bible, a vase, a pen and a book; by the table was a golden chair; there was also a wonderful golden chest and a golden bed. In each room there was a crown with jewels set into it, a golden harp and a trumpet. The walls were gold. From the Bible, which was made of a type of paper they had never seen on earth and bound with gold, such a brilliant light and glory shone out that they did not need any other light. The visitors were told that when they came to stay, after they had died, they could go out into Paradise and pick any flowers of their choice to put into the beautiful vase on the golden table.[5]

The children could go to their rooms whenever they wanted to, to read their Bibles or to play their harps and trumpets. Sometimes they took their trumpets or harps out into the streets or out into Paradise to play and sing with the angels and with the saints who had been saved by the blood of Jesus.

In these excursions through heaven the children, though lost to their real surroundings on earth, were always conscious that their visit to heaven was temporary. They knew they were there only to see what was prepared for them after death, so that they could go back to earth again and tell others. The angels and the Lord told the heavenly visitors that, if they believed and obeyed, all these things would be theirs. They not only knew they must come back to earth again, but they sometimes knew when they would return.

One boy, after enjoying the glories of heaven, hung his crown and trumpet up in his room so he could have them again after he died and went to heaven to stay there for ever. He then came back to earth and the power of the Holy Spirit left him. When he opened his eyes he was in our room at Adullam telling us about this wonderful trip to heaven.

Are we to imagine that the Lord saved these boys, baptized them in the Holy Spirit, and then fooled them by showing them a figurative and mythical heaven? Impossible! Our heavenly Father shows His children what He has for them (1 Corinthians 2:10), promises He will give them these things (Revelation 3:21), and then gives them the very thing He has promised (Luke 11:9, 13).

When the children saw the heavenly rooms of their Adullam friends they clapped their hands, laughed and shouted with great joy, calling one another by name to come and see the room. In the Spirit one of the children ran along the street of the New Jerusalem, reading out the names above each door.

Old friends in heaven

On the first day when the Holy Spirit fell upon the children, and one of the boys was caught up into heaven in a vision, along with the angels who came to welcome him, were two boys from Adullam who had died the year before and were without a doubt saved. These two, Hsi Dien Fu and Djang Hsing, had with them a little girl who had died in Kotchiu four years previously, whom our children had forgotten. The two boys who had died led the Adullam children around heaven, first of all to see Jesus and worship and thank Him, and then later to their rooms and then around the city and out into Paradise to play.

Everyone who went to heaven was given white garments. The angels, also dressed in seamless garments of spotless white, had wings, but those who had been saved did not. There was a clear distinction between the two.

Later on many more of the children saw these Adullam boys who are in heaven. Heaven did not seem far away as they acted out these heavenly visions before our eyes. With closed eyes and radiant faces, they clapped their hands and shouted for joy to these boys who had died the previous year, calling them to hurry over to see some room or some golden street, some new scene among the angels, some new discovery in the garden of Paradise, or to come and play the harp and sing with them the praises of Jesus. The boys who had died were seen so often in heaven and their names were shouted with such delight and joy that they did not seem far away, just out of sight. Heaven was so real, so near, so wonderful, so certain, that if one of our children had died in those days the others would have envied him the privilege.

The step to heaven after death or at the coming of the Lord seemed so small and the coming of the Lord so near that it removed from our minds all mystery as to why the first disciples could sell their possessions and face persecution and death without wavering.

Our Kingdom does not belong to this world. Our citizenship is in heaven and it is from there that we await our Saviour. Our life, or work, our service, our hardships here are only brief and passing incidents on the way to the true life, the true city, in the true Kingdom that cannot be shaken.

Notes

1. Paul writes in 2 Corinthians 12:2: *'I know a man in Christ who fourteen years ago was caught up to the third heaven.'*
2. Other people who have had visions of heaven have spoken of the city being arranged in sevens. There also seems to be a series of plains. We must not suppose that in vision anyone has seen more than a fraction of heaven.

3. *'For the kingdom of God is ... righteousness, peace and joy in the Holy Spirit'* (Romans 14:17).
4. See John 4:23.
5. Soon after the publication of the first edition of this book the author received a letter from a woman in England saying that ten years previously both she and her son had had visions of this street and of these homes, confirming the details of the visions which the Adullam children had received.

   In a distant part of the Province of Yunan a tribes boy who did not know of these other visions also saw this street. Tribes people also confirmed the visions of the other parts of the New Jerusalem which the Adullam children had, with spacious parks and elaborate mansions.

Chapter 5

Paradise

Before we describe the children's wonderful visions of Paradise we want to show that what the children saw is in line with the Father's plans for His children, as revealed in His Word.

When the Lord created the first perfect human being and gave him a perfect bride to be at his side he planted a garden *'in the east, in Eden'*.

> *'And the Lord God made all kinds of trees grow out of the ground – trees that were pleasing to the eye and good for food. In the middle of the garden were the tree of life and the tree of the knowledge of good and evil.'*
>
> (Genesis 2:9)

So right at the beginning God planned for human beings to live in the beauty of nature. He gave Adam and Eve a beautiful home which He Himself had planned and planted. There was no sin, no sickness, no death; there were no thorns or thistles. It was a very different world to the one we know now. It was heaven on earth and human beings could have enjoyed life and happiness there forever.

When sin entered the world, it spoiled creation. Eden and creation were no longer eternal: they became limited by time. Because of sin human beings lost their Eden and the relationship they enjoyed with God.

When human beings are restored they will return to their Eden paradise and to their relationship with God, but it will not be a return to the way things were at creation: a new spiritual order will be established.

The Garden of Eden was a paradise on earth; the Paradise to come is spiritual. But it is just as **real**. After He was resurrected Christ was real and similar to the way He was before, but at the same time He was spiritual and different. He could still eat and drink with His disciples.[1] He had a body which could be touched and hands that could serve fish and bread to His hungry disciples.[2] But in His resurrection body the Lord was not limited by the time and space of the material world.

Christ's resurrection from the dead not only saved fallen human beings: it saved creation too. One day our world with its animals, birds and plants will be reborn. It will be similar to the first creation but it will also be different. No longer will it be subject to corruption and decay. This will be the real order.

> *'The creation waits in eager expectation for the sons of God to be revealed. ... the creation itself will be liberated from its bondage to decay and brought into the glorious freedom of the children of God.'* (Romans 8:19, 21)

So nature and all plant and animal life look forward to being set free. The Bible tells us that those who have been saved by Christ are the 'first fruits' of the resurrection life that is to come for the whole of creation.[3]

Christ Himself is *'the image of the invisible God, the firstborn over all creation'* (Colossians 1:18). How can this be true unless the animal and plant kingdom will eventually follow and share in this rebirth? Even the earth will take part in this process since *'in keeping with his promise we are looking forward to a new heaven and a new earth, the home of righteousness'* (2 Peter 2:13). Surely this new earth will have trees and flowers, animals and birds and all the beauty of nature, but they will last forever. On that new earth:

'The wolf will live with the lamb,
the leopard will lie down with the goat,
the calf and the lion and the yearling together;
and a little child will lead them.' (Isaiah 11:6)

These things are as certain as the Word of God for:

'He who was seated on the throne said, "I am making everything new!" Then he said, "Write this down for these words are trustworthy and true."' (Revelation 21:5)

John *'saw a new heaven and a new earth'*, and he also *'saw the Holy City, the new Jerusalem, coming down out of heaven'* to the new earth (Revelation 21:1, 2).

Just as there was a Garden of Eden on the first earth full of pleasures and delights, so in the New Jerusalem there will be a New Eden. It is already in heaven in the New Jerusalem but it has not come down yet. But it is coming soon. Perhaps this idea will be as new to most of our readers as it was to us. This is because we are so slow to believe what the Scriptures tell us.

We did not teach the children about this Paradise. They taught us. Some of the smallest children, who in the natural knew the least about these matters, were our best teachers. If you compare what they saw with the teaching of the Bible, it is clear that they discovered these truths from the Lord.

The words 'Paradise' and 'Eden' have the same meaning. 'Paradise' is a Persian word which is used in the Septuagint to translate 'Eden'. 'Eden' means 'a park' – a place where people can enjoy themselves surrounded by fields and trees. But even the most beautiful parks on earth, with picturesque landscapes, streams, woodland, lovely meadows, flowers, birds and animals, are only pale imitations of the original Garden of Eden. The natural beauty we enjoy so much is a reminder of the Eden that awaits us at the end of our pilgrim journey.

The Adullam children see Paradise

You will be interested as we were in what our Adullam children saw in Paradise. One of the young men found himself in Paradise almost as soon as he entered the heavenly city. There he was met by the two Adullam boys who had died in Hokow. They soon came to a great open space like a huge lawn, surrounded by magnificent trees, which were golden and sparkling. The whole scene was so captivating that the young man said to his heavenly friends: 'This is good enough for me. There can't be anything more beautiful than this. I'll stay right here.' But the boys said, 'No, don't stay here. There are even more amazing things to see.' They went a little further and came to some even more magnificent trees, some of them bearing fruit. Again, it was so beautiful that we couldn't begin to imagine it. The young man said, 'I must stay here. I can't go on and leave this great beauty. I am so happy.' But again the boys encouraged him, 'Come on. There are far more beautiful places to see than this.' But he replied, 'You go. I'll stay here for a while.' They left him on the smooth, velvety grass under the trees with the great open space in front of him. On earth he had never known such joy and happiness as he knew then.

An angel came walking by, playing a harp and singing. The angel smiled and offered him the harp. 'I can't play,' he said. The angel went on. Soon other angels came, smiling to him as they played and sang.

The angels wore white seamless garments. Their faces were perfect and one was no more beautiful than another. 'When they smiled – oh, that is impossible to describe,' said the boy. 'There is no way on earth to describe an angel's smile.'

Similar scenes, and even more beautiful ones, were seen over and over again by the Adullam children. They saw trees bearing the most delicious fruit; they saw fields of the most amazing flowers of every shape and colour, giving off the most wonderful fragrance. There were birds with the most glorious plumage and fantastic song. There were also animals of every size and description: large deer, small deer, lions, elephants, rabbits and all sorts of little friendly pets such as they had never seen before.

The children held the pets in their arms and passed them from one to another. Or perhaps they found the lion lying peacefully under a tree. Then they climbed on his back, ran their fingers through his shaggy mane, brushed his face with their hands, and put their hands in his mouth. If they wanted to, they curled down beside him to enjoy the love of their Creator. As we have already seen,

> *'The wolf will live with the lamb,*
> *the leopard will lie down with the goat,*
> *the calf and the lion and the yearling together;*
> *and a little child will lead them.'* (Isaiah 11:6)

Little children rode on the small deer while older children rode the larger deer or a friendly elephant. It was a place of perfect love and harmony, full of joy and laughter. Only our Father in heaven could have planned such a Paradise!

When the children were hungry they simply picked the wonderful fruit that grew there or ate the sweet and refreshing manna they found scattered all about. If they were thirsty they drank the water of life from the little streams that trickled here and there through the garden.[4]

The Bible saints

On the wide open spaces, like huge lawns, groups of the heavenly people would gather and dance and play trumpets with the angels. Sometimes the Adullam children would join in the fun, along with the children, young people and adults, but no one was old. There was so much happiness and joy.

The angels pointed out Abraham, David, Daniel, the prophets and other Bible saints, and those believers who had been martyred. They saw Peter, James, Paul and others of whom the world was not worthy. One of our boys, from the poor Miao tribe, saw his aunt and his own little sister who had died. Our own little Chinese Mary, who died in Kotchiu, joined our boys and took them by the hand.

A vision of a Christian's death

In his vision the boy saw relatives and friends gathered around the bed of the person who was dying, while an angel stood by waiting for the man's spirit to be set free. When the time came the angel took the Christian by the hand and led him up to heaven. Evil principalities and powers tried to hinder their progress to heaven but they were overcome by the angel's faith and praise as they made their way to the heavenly city.

Having been welcomed at the gate, the new arrival was received by a great many angels, singing and dancing with tremendous joy, and together they gave him a royal welcome to the eternal city.

Notes

1. Acts 10:41–2.
2. Luke 24:39, 42; John 21:9, 31.
3. *'He chose to give us birth through the word of truth, that we might be a kind of firstfruits of all he created'* (James 1:18).
4. The Scriptures teach that there will be eating and drinking in the Kingdom of God: *'so that you may eat and drink at my table in my kingdom . . . '* (Luke 22:30); *'I tell you, I will not drink of this fruit of the vine from now on until that day when I drink it anew with you in my Father's kingdom'* (Matthew 26:29). The Bible also specifically says that there will be eating in the heavenly Paradise (Revelation 2:7). The 'tree of life' is a general term that covers a variety of fruit-bearing trees, the fruit having a life-giving quality which is particularly suited to human beings in their sinless state. The tree of life is not just one tree with one type of fruit, cf. *'And on either side of the river was the tree of life, bearing twelve kinds of fruit, yielding its fruit every month; and the leaves of the tree were for the healing of the nations'* (Revelation 22:1, 2 NASV).

Chapter 6

In the Presence of Angels

Whenever the children experienced the Holy Spirit in power they became acutely aware of the presence of angels.

Angels play an important role in the work of the Holy Spirit. According to 1 Corinthians 14:32 they are involved in words of prophecy in some way. John was given his visions on Patmos by an angel (Revelation 1:1, 10). Visions and prophecy are therefore key areas in which angels are involved.

The Bible suggests that each true church has a special angel which ministers to it (Revelation 1:20) as does every person who is saved (Hebrews 1:14; Acts 12:15). Every child is under the direct protection of an angel with constant access to the throne of God in heaven (Matthew 18:10). Despite the fact that we rarely see angels, they always see us.[1] There are different ranks of angels.

There is enough proof in both the Old and New Testaments to confirm that the angels the children at Adullam saw were real. We have already described the visions the children had of angels rescuing children who were being dragged to hell by demons. It would seem then that angels help to save the lost. Since angels led the children to heaven and escorted them through the streets of Paradise it would appear that they have something to do with the visions the children were given at Adullam. As most of the children who spoke in other languages did so when they were dancing and singing with the angels it may be that angels have something to do with speaking in other languages, for according to 1 Corinthians 1:13 it is possible to speak with the *'tongues of angels'*.

The children also had wonderful visions of large numbers of angels flying in the heavens, and sometimes they saw them fly from heaven to earth.

Angels at Adullam

At times when the presence of the Holy Spirit was there in power, the children saw angels actually in the room or nearby. When they felt under attack by demons they saw angels come to rescue them.

On occasions when there was a very strong sense of the presence of the Lord bringing deep harmony and love into the meeting, the children saw a large angel above the room and many smaller angels standing side by side, each touching the other to the right and left, entirely surrounding the room so there was no space left for any demon to creep in. On these occasions, when one or more children saw the troop of angels guarding us, there were never any visions of demons in the room, as on other occasions was frequently the case. One evening when the angel guard surrounded us in perfect rank the children said they could hear demons outside the circle making an angry commotion because they were thwarted in this way. This circle of angels was also seen by the boys in Kotchiu.

I shall never forget the amazing sense of the presence of God that was in those meetings when the children saw the angel watching over us. This angel looked down on us smiling and turned from side to side to look at the circle of angels surrounding us to make sure there was no possible entry point for the powers of darkness. I wondered if the angel above us was Adullam's special angel and if the smaller angels of lesser rank were our individual guardian angels. At any rate, the children saw the angels. Their eyes were usually closed when they saw them, but sometimes they saw them with their eyes wide open. We could believe without question that we were indeed in the presence of angels.

Note

1. 1 Corinthians 4:9.

Chapter 7

The Kingdom of the Devil

> *'For our struggle is not against flesh and blood, but against the rulers, against the authorities, against the powers of this dark world and against the spiritual forces of evil in the heavenly realms.'* (Ephesians 6:12)

No one who was with us during those weeks of the outpouring of the Holy Spirit could have failed to observe that there are two Kingdoms in constant conflict. One Kingdom became as real to us as the other, and without any shadow of a doubt human beings were the battleground. Both the Old and the New Testaments teach the reality of a Kingdom of darkness and of the existence of demons.

We have already told of how demons were cast out of one man and how the larger demon was seen angrily rushing about the room until finally he overcame the schoolteacher. On that occasion two boys said that the demon looked like a man but was big and black. When the demon was cast out of this victim by a Spirit-filled young man, several children saw him and the other demon, about half his size, take temporary refuge behind some trees in the courtyard of the house. Both demons were visible to the children, some of whom were praying with their eyes closed and some with their eyes open. But they all saw the same thing at the same time. The demons looked the same to all the children.

In the Adullam Rescue Home we had a young girl who was very evidently vulnerable to demon activity. She said that before coming here she was subject to 'fits', or spells of unconsciousness. A short time after her arrival she and some of the other girls went for a walk outside the city. On the way back one of the new girls who was half-blind and mentally disabled lingered behind and lost her way. The older girl, having gone to find the one who was lost, was returning home with her when she saw three demons in front of her. One was 'as tall as a door' and was accompanied by two others about the size of a twelve-year-old boy. They were all dark in appearance, with big eyes and awful faces. The two smaller demons seemed under the control of the large one, and obeyed and followed him. The girl was terrified. The large demon came up to her and seized her by the head. She became dizzy and almost unconscious, and could scarcely walk. She could hardly see the street and had to be led home by the other girl whom she had gone to find. When they arrived home she felt better for a while, but a little later, while we were at supper, someone came in to tell us she was in her room unconscious. We found her lying on the floor, breathing as if in a peaceful sleep, but we could not wake her. After praying for her we all went as usual to our evening prayer meeting. The girl soon came in perfectly well.

She told us what had happened. She felt as if she was in chains and was being dragged by the demons, further and further down a long dark road; all the time she kept praying silently. Then she suddenly realized that the Lord had set her free and she was able to get up. At once she regained consciousness, and her mind became clear. As she sat on her bed alone, she saw the three demons in the room. But now she felt no fear, for she knew that the Lord was Conqueror. She drove the demons out of the room 'in the name of Jesus'. As they reluctantly left step by step she followed in the name of Jesus until she drove them along the walkway out of the large Chinese door at the entrance of our compound. In the next few months that she was with us she had no more 'fits' or unconscious spells.

I have given these two incidents in detail because in both cases the effect of the demon activity was so clear that any observer would have known that something supernatural had taken place. There are many other stories we could tell, but these two are sufficient in this connection. We want to talk now about the demonic activity that went side by side with the activity of the Holy Spirit.

When there were manifestations of the Holy Spirit we did not understand we kept praying and trusting the Lord but decided not to interfere unless we saw something that was clearly harmful or sinful. After eight weeks of extraordinary Holy Spirit activity we were deeply thankful that we had allowed the children this freedom. We saw how amazingly the Lord had led them, and things we did not understand at first proved to be part of the Lord's plan in giving us some of the most wonderful and precious revelations.

Demons

While some of the children were being really blessed by the Holy Spirit, others kept falling asleep when they tried to pray. Those under the anointing of the Holy Spirit could often see demons by those who were drowsy and could not break through. Sometimes they saw demons coming in through the open window or the door or lying lazily under the table or a couch that was in the room. Under the anointing of the Holy Spirit, the children, with their eyes closed, would force the demons out of these places and would follow them until they went out of the door or window. They frequently followed these demons out of the room, opened a front or back door to the compound, and chased the demons off the premises. When demons appeared on the scene they were often seen by several people at the same time.

Some of the children had seen demons before. We found out that, despite all our teaching about the Lord, they were still so afraid of demons that they dared not go to their room alone at night, and they put their blankets over their heads when they slept. Through their experiences of the Holy Spirit, however, the children discovered that even the largest and most terrifying demons had no power over even the smallest child protected by the blood of Jesus. For the first time we had a happy bunch of Chinese children who lost their fear of demons, were not afraid in the dark and were able to sleep with their heads uncovered.

You may be wondering what demons look like. They resemble the demon idols in Chinese temples. According to the Bible[1] and to the Chinese much idolatry is demon worship, and the idols are human beings' attempts to reproduce the likenesses of demons that have been seen.

The children saw demons as 'tall as a door', with pointed chins and heads covered with warts. Some were half this size, while others were just two or three feet; others were just two or three inches high and followed the larger demons around. The large, fierce-looking demons with big eyes are the ones to be feared as they have the power to take people prisoner and drag them off to hell.

Principalities and powers

Under the anointing of the Holy Spirit the children at Adullam found out that the principalities and powers of darkness work in co-operation with the demons on earth. This is what they discovered.

The seat of government of the evil powers is in the mid-heavens. Here the devil's angels have their thrones and exercise their satanic government over the earth. Their appearance, size, dress, disposition and authority vary. In all respects they are as devilish in both appearance and activity as you would expect them to be.

These evil rulers argue constantly among themselves, each jealously resenting the authority of those with greater power and higher in rank. Those higher in rank hold onto their positions not by the consent of those lower down but only through their own greater fierceness and power. There are constant quarrels and in-fighting.

The angels all wear crowns representing various orders and ranks. They all want to sit on the thrones and supervise the work of evil on earth, rather than have to go down to earth on delegated duties and actually carry out the work. The higher-ranked demonic powers sit on the thrones in mid-heaven, ruling over the countless numbers of evil spirits, constantly despatching delegations to oppose the forces of righteousness, to strengthen the weak spots in the demonic forces on earth, and to drag people off to hell when they die.

Although the devil's angels fly in high heaven right up to the gates of the New Jerusalem and although they come to earth and fly in its air, they congregate in their thousands in the mid-heavens where the thrones of authority are. Here evil spirits of all sizes fly backwards and forwards, and move about for one purpose or another. The angels of higher rank have a kind of halo.

In some respects they are all similar: they all have wings, they all have crowns and they all belong in the heavens. The messengers only go to earth temporarily until their evil errand is completed, and then they return to the heavens again.

The thousands of evil spirits on the earth are very different from the devil's angels. They do not have wings; they can walk and run very quickly; they move about freely but they do not seem to leave the earth. They vary in size from a few inches to ten feet in height, wear gaudy striped clothes, and wear caps of various shapes and colours; other types of demons wear rags or filthy clothes.

Some of these demons that live on the earth have very little power and are quite harmless. Others, however, are large, fierce and very powerful. They oppose the work of men and women who love God, and His angels. In a vision the children saw one of their conflicts with an angel: the highest ranked demons on the earth, helped by those of lower rank, surrounded the angel and tried to strike him with clubs, swords and other weapons. Through faith and praising the Lord, the angel was able to survive the attack without suffering any blows or physical assault. The less powerful demons stood a little distance away, watching the fight; seeing that their companions were not having any success they prayed to the powers of evil in the heavens to send a reinforcement of the devil's angels from the air. In response, a detachment of ten angels was sent down. As they approached the earth the demons clapped their hands to welcome them. When the satanic angels reached the scene of conflict the less powerful demons stood a little way away in respectful silence, while they took up the conflict. The angel continued to praise the Lord and to stand in faith and was able to resist their attack, until suddenly the glory of God came down and the evil forces were completely dispersed.

Visions of a non-Christian's death

When a man who had not heard the gospel died, his spirit was set free from his body and wandered about from place to place on the earth, until one of the devil's angels, coming down from the sky, put him in chains and forced him down to hell.

The death of a professing Christian who had known the Lord but had fallen away from faith was even more terrifying. Demons lay in wait by the bedside of this dying man, eagerly awaiting the moment of death. Before he had even died, they began to put the chains on him. The moment he gave his last breath they took his spirit prisoner and dragged the terrified man off to hell. His spirit did not have a moment's freedom to wander the earth.

In another vision demons were seen taunting the spirit of a man who had turned away from God. As they dragged him along in chains, again and again they jerked him to his feet before forcing him to the ground again and hauling him along like a dead dog. When they at last tired of their cruel fun they took him down the dark road to hell.

One boy had come to the Adullam Rescue Home after living on the streets for several days. He had been an errand boy for the army but had been discharged because of his bad behaviour. He promised to change his ways and so we took him in. For a while he seemed to make a go of it. He heard the gospel and said he had repented.

Then different articles disappeared from the Home. At first we did not know who the thief was, but later the boy was discovered on his way to sell the goods. We put him out of the Home.

He lived as a beggar for several months and during this time he repeatedly promised to change if only we would give him a second chance. This we did. The Lord also gave him another chance, allowing him to experience manifestations of the Holy Spirit and supernatural revelations, which would have convinced even the simplest person of the ways of God. The boy himself had experiences of the Holy Spirit's anointing when the Lord dealt with him directly about his sins and showed him a better way of living. In spite of all this the boy ran away and joined a street gang of beggar-thieves. A few months later he fell and broke his arm, and was picked up by a hospital worker. In the hospital he was so hopelessly disobedient that he was thrown out, and was soon on the verge of death on the street. He came to us with more promises of repentance and we took him in again.

He became more and more seriously ill. The night before he died I was wakened by some devilish shrieks that sounded like the howls of a wild animal or some fiend from hell. The next day when the boy died, I was away from home. As he lay dying demons surrounded him in eager anticipation. When his spirit was leaving his body the boy shrieked, wept, yelled and cried at the top of his voice in utter terror: 'Mr Baker, help! help! help! Oh, Mr Baker, come quickly! Mr Baker, Mr Baker, Mr Baker! Help, they are all around me with chains! They have come for me. Help, help, Mr Baker, help! Oh, oh, oh, help! help! help!

They're putting me in chains. Help! help! Oh, oh, oh, help! Oh h-e-l-!'

Visions of hell

Over and over again children had visions of hell and the lake of fire. Usually, the first time anyone came under the anointing of the Holy Spirit they saw a vision of hell. In their vision they were taken in chains through a very dark region. It was always pitch-black. Some children could hear demons all around them. After travelling a long time some could see a dim light in the distance which turned out to be reflections from the lake of fire. Some children were forced to go so close that they could see the lake of fire ahead of them. All the time they were calling on the blood of Jesus and declaring that they would not obey and would not allow themselves to be made the slaves of their evil captors. They believed Jesus would surely save them. As we have already related, at this crucial moment the Lord did indeed intervene and save them by His blood.

The Bible pictures hell as a place of blackest darkness (see, for example, 2 Peter 2:17), and it teaches that some of the devil's angels are already in chains awaiting judgement (see Jude 6).

The lake of fire

The children were led to the edge of a lake of molten fire from which clouds of smoke billowed up. When the smoke settled low over the lake, the fire was less distinct. When it lifted a little, the burning lake could be seen clearly, with its red and greenish flames and its prisoners.

When, in their vision, the children were peering down into the pit, they would grab hold of a piece of furniture, or get down on their hands and knees, cautiously bending forward to take a look. After a moment they drew back again, afraid that they might fall in. They were absolutely horrified by what they saw. Then very cautiously they looked again before turning away. Sometimes the children lay flat on their stomachs, afraid they might slip and fall while looking over the edge into the lake of fire.

They saw the lost going into hell. Some fell in, some walked over the edge and some were thrown in in chains by demons. One boy saw a number of people tied up together in bundles, ready to be thrown into this fire (cf. Matthew 13:47–50).

When the fire burnt down and the smoke settled, they could hear moans. At intervals the intensity of the fire increased and these became shrieks and wails of agony.

In a vision one person rolled on the floor in agony, crying out as those suffering in hell would do.

Oceans of hands reached up out of the fire for help, appealing to those looking down to come to their rescue. We could hear the children talking to them just as you get just one end of a telephone conversation. They said: 'I can't help you.' 'No, I can't do anything for you.' 'But when you were alive you would not obey the gospel.' 'No, it is too late; before you got here I preached to you, but you made fun of me and despised Jesus. Now you know I told you the truth.' 'No, I can't do anything; this is the judgement of God.' 'If you had obeyed, you would now be enjoying heaven with us.' After a while the children were led away to enjoy the presence of Jesus in heaven or the wonders of Paradise.

In the Gospel of Luke Lazarus could see the rich man in hell tormented by the flames:

> *'In hell, where he was in torment, he looked up and saw Abraham far away, with Lazarus by his side. So he called to him, "Father Abraham, have pity on me and send Lazarus to dip the tip of his finger in water and cool my tongue, because I am in agony in this fire." But Abraham replied, "Son, remember that in your lifetime you received your good things, while Lazarus received bad things, but now he is comforted here and you are in agony. And besides all this, between us and you a great chasm has been fixed,*

> *so that those who want to go from here to you cannot, nor can anyone cross over from there to us."'*
>
> (Luke 16:23–6)

One boy saw his grandmother in hell, whom he had tried to win to Christ. She was a sorceress and a murderer, and had been very resistant to the gospel, causing many others in her village to refuse to believe. (This boy was the one who met his little sister and aunt in heaven.) Other children also saw visions of their relatives in hell.

The people in hell were all those who did not believe and trust in the name of Jesus. One night when the Lord spoke through a small boy in wonderful prophecy, among the things he said was, 'There will be no one in heaven except those who believe the gospel.'

The crossroads

Through the Holy Spirit the Lord taught the boys and girls many lessons in a quite systematic way. One particular vision was repeated so often it seemed it could never be forgotten. The person in the vision was standing by the cross at a place where two roads parted. One road was the narrow way of life that leads to heaven and glory; the other was the wide road to hell and destruction.

Crowds and crowds of people were hurrying along – hustling and bustling with business, carrying great loads of sin and rushing along preoccupied with all the affairs of life. The child was a preacher at the crossroads. Again we heard one side of the conversation: 'Hello, my friend. Please wait a minute; I want to speak to you. Don't go down that wide road: it leads to hell and ruin. I have been down that way and have seen hell for myself. Stop here by the cross and let Jesus take all your sins away. From the cross of Christ here you can start going up this other road that will lead you to heaven and everlasting life and joy. Oh! That person doesn't believe it – there he goes down the wide road. What a pity! I'll stop this other man and see if he will believe. Hey there! Just a minute! Don't follow that crowd! They don't know where they're going. That road leads to destruction; it leads to the lake of fire. Please don't go that way. I came out here to stop as many of you as possible and give you fair warning. Better stop here and let Jesus take your sins away. Go with us up the road to heaven, where God is. Oh, there he goes, too!

Here's someone else. Wait a moment! Leave the crowd! Can't you see there is no one travelling back that way? They all go down that road; no one ever comes back. That is the wide road to hell. Stop here by the cross, believe that you can be saved through the blood of Jesus, and you will be safe. There is no other road further on. This is the only road to heaven. Turn in here or you will be lost too. Oh, she doesn't believe me either. There she goes with the others.'

Sometimes the young preacher decided that if no one believed him he would follow the stubborn crowd to see what happened. When he arrived with the crowd at the brink of the lake of fire we heard him say, 'Look at that crowd falling into hell. No one escapes. I told you about this back there at the crossroads, but you would not believe. Now I can't do anything to help you. If you had listened back there, when I warned you, the Lord would have saved you. You wouldn't take my advice. Now, I can't help you. I'm going back to the crossroads to see if I can find someone who will listen. I must see if I can stop at least someone.'

Occasionally he was successful in persuading someone to listen. Then he would say, 'Now, you kneel down there at the foot of the cross of Jesus and pray. Oh, you don't know how to pray? Well, say what I tell you. "Jesus, I am a sinner! I was on the road to hell. I am only fit for hell. This big load I'm carrying is my sin. Forgive my sins and teach me to live only for Your glory. Amen."' There was great joy as the sinner was saved. As that person set off down the narrow road, the preacher went out to try to rescue someone else heading for destruction.

This vision, with some variations, was repeated many times, making the truths of salvation very clear. Jesus had warned:

> *'Enter through the narrow gate. For wide is the gate and broad is the road that leads to destruction, and many enter through it. But small is the gate and narrow the road that leads to life, and only a few find it.'*
>
> (Matthew 7:13–14)

The vision also emphasized that Christians are to stand in the gap for those hurtling towards hell, and warn and persuade to the very limits of their ability.

The visions, as I mentioned in a previous chapter, prompted the boys to go out onto the streets with the message of the gospel. From the youngest to the oldest they preached under the power of the Holy Spirit and were sometimes given such direct inspiration that I was amazed – I had never witnessed anything like it before.

The university student

Opposite our front gate lived a university student who was due to graduate later that year. Soon after he moved in I spoke to him, inviting him to come over and spend an informal evening discussing the Bible and Christianity with us. He came a few times, and I felt certain he was convinced of the truth of what I said. He seemed to be satisfied with my answers to his questions. Through him I managed to get a chance to talk to some of the other university students during their vacations. Ten days after I started going to see them in their rooms, we experienced the move of the Holy Spirit at Adullam.

The students were friendly, and I felt that the first undergraduate we had met was clearly convinced of the truth of the gospel, but, although he was polite, he did not want to believe it. He didn't seem to like the friendly way the other students responded to the Bible discussions.

One morning one of our girls bumped into the university student at our front gate. The girl began telling him he ought to become a Christian, in a simple way urging him to believe in Jesus to save him.

'What's the use of my being a Christian?' he asked. 'I don't need to be saved.'

'You might die suddenly, and then you would go to hell.'

'Who are you?' scoffed the student. 'You are a little snip of an ignorant girl, a useless beggar. What do you suppose you are up to? You are trying to teach me something when you are not even worthy to talk to me. I am a university student. I am wise. I have read many books. I have been in Peking for many years. I can speak and read English as well as Chinese.' He then spat in her face and told her to mind her own business.

Two weeks later I heard the commotion of a funeral in the front alley. I was dismayed to learn that they were carrying this student to his burial – I had seen him on the street only a few days ago. One of the boys said that a few days earlier, as we were going out to preach, he had offered this young man a tract but he would not take it. I knew nothing of his conversation with the girl.

About a month later this girl was in a trance under the power of the Spirit. After seeing glorious visions of heaven she stood still and bent over as if she were looking into hell. Then we heard her say: 'Ah, there is hell. No, I cannot. I have no power to help you now. I can see you are in an awful situation. It is you who are worse than a beggar now, all dirty, filthy and suffering in the lake of fire. In fact, you look worse now than any beggar I ever saw. I thought you told me you were rich and that you had a great education. Where is your education now? Well, I can't help you, even if you do apologize. I have no power. Only Jesus can save you, but when I told you about Him you made fun of Him and cursed me.

'Look what we beggars have received in Jesus: in heaven there is wonderful joy, happiness and love. We will enjoy the Paradise of God forever.'

It is hard to be saved

Then the girl seemed to be crossing the lake of fire over a narrow bridge. We saw her walking as if she were on a tightrope, placing one foot carefully in front of the other holding her arms out on both sides to keep her balance. With a sigh of relief she said, 'This is so dangerous! But with the Lord's help I will get across to the other side.' Then she carefully brought the other foot forward and nearly lost her balance again. She praised the Lord until she recovered her balance and went on as before. She crossed the room in this way until she seemed to be safely in heaven, and past every danger of falling into the lake of fire.

Whatever the effect of relating these visions may have on others, they served to convince us more than ever of the reality of heaven and the Kingdom of God, and of the reality of hell and the Kingdom of the devil. It is clearer to us than ever before that it is not easy to get to heaven: it is like walking step by step on a tightrope. Only Jesus can stop us from falling. The Scriptures tell us:

> *'For it is time for judgement to begin with the family of God; and if it begins with us, what will the outcome be for those who do not obey the gospel of God? And, "If it is hard for the righteous to be saved, what will become of the ungodly and the sinner?"'* (1 Peter 4:17, 18)

We are surer than ever that God means for us to stand at the crossroads at the foot of the cross to point sinners to the narrow road that leads to salvation.

Note

1. 1 Corinthians 10:20.

Chapter 8

The End of the Age and the Return of Christ

> *'They will see the Son of Man coming on the clouds of the sky, with power and great glory.'* (Matthew 24:30)

Through the visions and prophecies that the Holy Spirit gave us we were warned repeatedly that the end of the present age and the return of the Lord are very near. The Holy Spirit made this truth so vivid and so real to us that there was no doubt in any of our minds about how important this message was.

Jesus told a parable about a farmer who planted his field with good seed, but his enemy came and sowed weeds among the wheat, so that when the wheat grew it was mixed with weeds. Rather than pull out the weeds and risk destroying the wheat the farmer waited until the harvest time to deal with the weeds (see Matthew 13:24–30, 36–43). Just as in this parable, the Lord showed us that the end of the earth will come – the harvest – when the Kingdom of the devil is at its worst and the Kingdom of God on earth is at its best, in its purest form. The Bible also teaches that evil will reach its climax through an evil world ruler who is possessed by the devil – indeed an incarnation of the devil himself. This superman will be destroyed by the Lord at His return.[1]

There may be those who take exception to these remarks, but, without discussing them in detail, I will relate, as best I can, the visions and revelations given to the Adullam children, who knew little or nothing of end-time theology.

Disease and wars

Time after time the children prophesied that a time of famine, disease, war and desolation is coming. During this time the people of God will be persecuted but God will equip and protect them through the crisis. The Scriptures refer to this time as the Great Tribulation.

One boy saw our schoolteacher trying to buy some rice. There was such a huge crowd surrounding the granary that the teacher had to push with the crowd in order to have any hope of being successful. Each person was permitted to buy only one measure of rice.

One uneducated boy was transported in a vision to our 'civilised' countries and saw people preparing for war, making bombs and other weapons of destruction.

Visions of the devil and the Antichrist

The children were given visions of the devil as a dragon with seven heads. One boy saw angels fighting with him and seven of his angels. The devil and his angels were overcome and thrown out of heaven to the earth.[2]

Adullam boys and girls saw visions of the superman the world is hoping for – the subject of worship of many of the world's religions. They saw the devil take the form of a strong handsome man, in the peak of his manhood, and come to earth as the Antichrist.

They also had visions of the image which, according to biblical prophecy, the Antichrist will erect as an object of worship, the image that will be able to speak and to deceive the world.[3] I asked them how they knew this handsome and powerful man was the Antichrist. They said that a great number of demons followed him wherever he went and obeyed his every command.

The Antichrist was also seen on a wide open plain as a great beast with seven heads. I asked them again how they knew this was the Antichrist, and the children said the angels told them. As I have already explained, these visions were given to the children, as they were to John, through angels while they were in a trance and, like him, they carried on a conversation with the angels who were able to explain to them many things they did not understand.

Those who love God are persecuted

During the terrifying reign of this evil superman those who loved God were standing firm and bearing witness to God despite great hardship and danger. The children saw that the two witnesses in Jerusalem and the Christians were given great supernatural power, in order to be able to resist and fight against the power of darkness during that awful time. There has never been a time on earth like it: the devil and all his angels, having been turned loose on the earth, will run riot and cause as much destruction and havoc as possible, because they know they only have a short time. At that time no one but a true Spirit-filled Christian will be able to stand even for one day against such satanic power which will demonstrate itself in supernatural miracles and manifestations.

But the children saw Christians filled with even greater supernatural power. They had visions of them preaching the gospel boldly in the face of great persecution with such power that, at a word from them, their enemies were struck down with plagues or death. They were moving in the power the Lord had promised His disciples:

> *'I tell you the truth, anyone who has faith in me will do what I have been doing. He will do even greater things than these, because I am going to the Father.'* (John 14:12)

In some cases, if a town rejected the gospel after Christians had witnessed in it, when they were some distance away, fire would fall from heaven and destroy it, as it had done at Sodom and Gomorrah. When persecution was particularly severe, they were sometimes carried away physically by the Holy Spirit, as Philip had been and as the prophets supposed Elijah had been.[4] In times of hunger and need manna, fruit and other food were miraculously provided, and angels ministered to them.

The Christians had the power to preach to tribes who had never heard the gospel in their own languages. We were able to glimpse how this might be true when in their visions the boys and girls were preaching in the Spirit. When one speaker preached to the people of a tribe whose language he or she did not know, another interpreted (cf. 1 Corinthians 14:28). Both spoke in other languages. One spoke a few sentences, then the other interpreted. They were preaching to people of every tribe and language.[5]

The children's visions of the gospel being preached in supernatural power seem to me to be in line with the prophecies in the Scriptures. I think we may well expect that, in the end days, the outpouring of the Holy Spirit will be far greater than what the first disciples experienced on the Day of Pentecost.

The final world war

At the conclusion of history, when there will be the most perfect and supernatural Church the world has ever seen and when there will be the greatest concentration of Satan's demonic power and devil-controlled human power that any age of earth has ever experienced, the Adullam children saw the Antichrist marshalling his forces for the final world war.

They also saw the war in the spirit realm. In these visions, they saw a man on a white horse leading an army of angels who were all dressed in white. They also saw a rider on a red horse: this rider was dressed in the most beautiful darkly coloured clothes and was followed by a large number of black demons.

They also received some visions of the war on earth. The children saw battleships being destroyed by bombs dropped from aeroplanes, with the loss of both the ships and all on board. They saw armies from all over the earth engaged in the most terrible conflicts. As the children stood and watched, they witnessed countless people being killed by poison gas and deadly instruments of war. At first the dead were buried, but as time went on there were too many dead bodies to cope with: they were piled up in great mounds or left to rot like manure, as the prophet had foretold they would.[6]

The sudden return of Christ

Everything was interrupted by Christ's sudden return. The sun became dark and the moon turned the colour of blood.[7] The stars fell out of the sky in great showers. The heavens shook and seemed to roll up like a scroll. There was a massive earthquake that ripped the earth apart. Great chasms appeared and people were swallowed alive. Because of the vigorous shaking houses just fell down, collapsing like dolls' houses, killing the inhabitants or burying them alive.

While these things were taking place in heaven and on earth the Lord appeared in the heavens. Old and young, rich and poor were overcome with a deadly fear and ran for their lives. People fled from their shops empty-handed, without a thought for the valuables that a few moments earlier had seemed so important. Families rushed from their homes without even a glance back at the luxuries that had been their life's passion. In that moment all men and women had only one purpose in mind: to run from the presence of the returning Judge; to find a place to hide from the King of kings. Some of those who managed to avoid the collapsing houses or who did not fall down the cracks in the earth tried to run to the mountains for safety; some jumped into the rivers and died; some killed themselves.

There was the sound of wails and shrieks everywhere. There was chaos and terror. Anything to escape from the anger of the Lamb, for the great day of His anger had come.

The great supper of God

> *'And I saw an angel standing in the sun, who cried in a loud voice to all the birds flying in mid-air, "Come, gather together for the great supper of God, so that you may eat the flesh of kings, generals, and mighty men, of horses and their riders, and the flesh of all people, free and slave, small and great."'* (Revelation 19:17, 18)

The birds and the animals were invited to eat the unburied corpses that lay scattered over the ruined earth. Birds, scavengers, wild animals and dogs were seen feeding on the carcasses.

While the children were witnessing this great feast we could hear their remarks and see their movements as the scene was described and acted out in front of us. One might say: 'Look at that eagle eating that rich man. It's picking his rich clothes off his body. Look at that! It has taken a piece of flesh and flown away.' Then another: 'Oh, look over there – a vulture and a crow both eating that man. The vulture has the most courage. He just picks and picks away, gorging himself, never taking time to look up, but the crow is afraid; he takes a bit and then looks around to see if he is in danger. Do you see that? Look at those birds standing on that well-dressed man and digging into him.'

Then the boys, as if in silent agreement, suddenly all turned their backs on the disgusting scene, making it clear by their actions as well as their words just how abhorrent these final scenes will be. The rich and mighty of the earth – the leaders among people, the business giants, the industrial magnates, the generals, the world religious leaders – will be there, not as honoured guests but as the food of the scavengers of the earth which they have exploited in their selfish luxury.

The Adullam children have seen and vividly described the terrible scenes that will mark the climax of our civilisation. They have witnessed the outcome of all our futile human endeavours. These simple children believe what is written in the Word of God without a doubt, because they have been shown it by God and His angels.

The fate of the Antichrist and the devil

The children saw the Lord and His angels putting chains around the hands and the feet of the Antichrist and preparing to throw him alive into hell.

There were also visions in which the devil was taken alive to the mouth of the pit of hell. A lid, like the lid of a box, opened and the devil was thrown down a black shaft of what looked like a well, into the abyss; the lid was closed, and the Lord locked it with a great key.[8]

Those who love God are taken to heaven

We have described how the return of Christ will affect those who have rejected Him. There were equally clear visions relating to those who love Him. The children saw the heavens open and the Lord come down in glory surrounded by all His angels. The angels heading up the procession blew beautiful trumpets, and those following on behind maintained perfect order, each one keeping in his proper place and rank. As the Lord descended towards the earth there were the most amazing scenes of graves bursting open as if there had been an explosion. Bodies coming out of the graves were suddenly transformed by resurrection life. In some cases bones were seen coming together (as the children expressed it in their Chinese idiom: 'one bone from the east and one from the west'). Now in their resurrection bodies these people were caught up to meet the Lord in the air.[9]

One boy saw a funeral procession taking a Christian to be buried. On the way to the burial ground the trumpet sounded and the Lord came down from heaven. The coffin opened, the dead man sat up and, as he was taken up into the air, his body was transformed.

I have already spoken of the children's visions of people we knew, dressed in white and enjoying Paradise, as well as of the heroes of the Bible. The Scriptures teach us that between death and the resurrection the saints have spiritual bodies and are clothed in white **before** the time of the resurrection.[10] I cross-questioned the children because I wanted to know how they knew whether the people they saw in heaven had resurrection bodies, or not. They said they did not know until the angels told them that they were only seeing these people's souls, not their bodies, which had not yet been resurrected. I questioned them over and over again on these matters, and always received the same answers: they always saw the people in heaven dressed in white; they never had wings; all the angels had wings; there was no difficulty in distinguishing between the people and the angels.

The wedding supper of the Lamb[11]

Great tables were laid out in Paradise among the magnificent trees, flowers, birds and animals. This place of indescribable beauty and harmony was filled with intense joy as the inhabitants of heaven and the angels praised the Lord, dancing, singing and playing trumpets and harps. Some of the children acted out these scenes in front of us. They hurried to their heavenly home to fetch their harp or trumpet before joining in the Spirit-inspired music in this greatest of all celebrations, the climax of all the hopes of the ages. Great choirs of people sang, danced and praised the King, while others hurried about preparing the tables or the seats, or carrying the golden plates of food. There was an abundance of food, everything having its own exquisite and unique flavour, and exceeding anything that could be imagined.

When everything was ready, the call went out and those who had been saved from every age gathered around the tables to celebrate the wedding of the King's Great Son. The greatest joy came when the rejects and outcasts from every corner of the earth – the beggars, the sinners, the prostitutes – sat down at this celebration feast with Abraham, Isaac and Jacob. Then came the moment everyone had been waiting for: the Son Himself came in and sat down at the tables where He was surrounded by the beautiful and pure Bride, which He had won with His own blood. Then He drank wine with them, as He had promised He would.[12]

The Day of Judgement

The children saw the Judge upon the throne and they saw too the books in which the actions of every man and woman are recorded. Those who had been saved by the death and resurrection of Jesus Christ were separated out from the crowd and stood together on one side, while those whose names were not in the Book of Life were gathered together on the other side. The one company was destined to enter the Kingdom of God and eternal life, while the other group was doomed to go into the fire prepared for the devil and his angels.[13]

The new heaven and the new earth

A few of the children were privileged to have visions of the new heaven and the new earth. The new heaven was so filled with *shekinah* glory that the children could not see it very distinctly.

The New Jerusalem occupied the central position in the new earth. They saw the heavenly city with its Paradise as it is now, but it had descended onto the new earth. The new earth was very like Paradise. It was the earth that God had intended for His children. It had been renewed[14] and will never pass away. On this earth God will live with His people again; He will be their God and they will be His people.

Notes

1. See 2 Thessalonians 2:1–10.
2. *'Then another sign appeared in heaven: an enormous red dragon with seven heads and ten horns and seven crowns on his heads. And there was war in heaven. Michael and his angels fought against the dragon, and the dragon and his angels fought back. But he was not strong enough, and they lost their place in heaven. The great dragon was hurled down – that ancient serpent called the devil or Satan, who leads the whole world astray. He was hurled to the earth, and his angels with him ... "But woe to the earth and the sea, because the devil has gone down to you! He is filled with fury, because he knows that his time is short"'* (Revelation 12:3, 7–9, 12).
3. *'He ordered them to set up an image in honour of the beast who was wounded by the sword and yet lived. He was given power to give breath to the image of the first beast, so that it could speak and cause all who refused to worship the image to be killed'* (Revelation 13:14b–15).
4. Acts 8:39; 2 Kings 2:16.
5. In his visions John saw: *'... another angel flying in mid-air, and he had the eternal gospel to proclaim to those who live on the earth – to every nation, tribe, language and people. He said in a loud voice, "Fear God and give him glory, because the hour of his judgment has come. Worship him who made the heavens, the earth, the sea and the springs of water"'* (Revelation 14:6–7); *'... there before me was a great multitude that no-one could count, from every nation, tribe, people and language, standing before the throne and in front of the Lamb. They were wearing white robes and were holding palm branches in their hands ... "These are they who have come out of the great tribulation; they have washed their robes and made them white in the blood of the Lamb"'* (Revelation 7:9, 14).
6. *'At that time those slain by the Lord will be everywhere – from one end of the earth to the other. They will not be mourned or gathered up or buried, but will be like refuse lying on the ground'* (Jeremiah 25:33).
7. *'Immediately after the distress of those days "the sun will be darkened, and the moon will not give its light; the stars will fall from the sky, and the heavenly bodies will be shaken"'* (Matthew 24:29). See also Revelation 6:12–17.
8. *'And I saw an angel coming down out of heaven, having the key to the Abyss and holding in his hand a great chain. He seized the dragon, that ancient serpent, who is the devil, or Satan, and bound him for a thousand years. He threw him into the Abyss, and locked and sealed it over him, to keep him from deceiving the nations any more until the thousand years were ended. After that, he must be set free for a short time'* (Revelation 20:1–3).

9. *'For the Lord himself will come down from heaven, with a loud command, with the voice of the archangel and with the trumpet call of God, and the dead in Christ will rise first. After that, we who are still alive and are left will be caught up with them in the clouds to meet the Lord in the air. And so we will be with the Lord for ever'* (1 Thessalonians 4:16–17).
10. *'When he opened the fifth seal, I saw under the altar the souls of those who been slain because of the word of God and the testimony they had maintained. They called out in a loud voice, "How long, Sovereign Lord, holy and true, until you judge the inhabitants of the earth and avenge our blood?" Then each of them was given a white robe, and they were told to wait a little longer, until the number of their fellow-servants and brothers who were to be killed as they had been was completed'* (Revelation 6:9–12).
11. *'Then the angel said to me, "Write: 'Blessed are those who are invited to the wedding supper of the Lamb!'" And he added, "These are the true words of God"'* (Revelation 19:9).
12. *'I tell you, I will not drink of this fruit of the vine from now on until that day when I drink it anew with you in my Father's kingdom'* (Matthew 26:29).
13. *'Then the King will say to those on his right, "Come, you who are blessed by my Father; take your inheritance, the kingdom prepared for you since the creation of the world." ... Then he will say to those on his left, "Depart from me, you who are cursed, into the eternal fire prepared for the devil and his angels"'* (Matthew 25:34, 41).
14. *'He who was seated on the throne said, "I am making everything new"'* (Revelation 21:5).

Chapter 9

Chinese Beggar Boy Prophesies

In fulfilment of the scripture that *'In the last days ... your sons and daughters will prophesy...'* (Acts 2:17), a ten-year-old boy was used by the Lord to bring us a message we will never forget.

A few months earlier this boy had been a beggar. He had arrived at our doorstep in rags and filthy – in fact with more dirt than clothes – with two other boys and asked if he might come in. When bathed and dressed the boy looked like an innocent chap, and so he proved to be. He at once took every Bible story and sermon to heart. He soon learned to pray, and we could hear him praying very earnestly every night. When the Holy Spirit came in power at Adullam this boy was among the first to receive baptism in the Holy Spirit and to speak in tongues.

Just as surely as God spoke to men and women in the past, making it possible for them to claim that the Scriptures were inspired by God and to declare, 'Thus says the Lord' with such conviction that they were willing to stake their lives on it, so God still speaks to His children today, when circumstances demand it and faith and other conditions permit it.

One night there was an unusually strong sense of the Lord's presence and heaven seemed very near. The boy I have just spoken about seemed to leave the earth and be caught up in heaven. Ushered into the presence of the Lord

Jesus he fell flat on his face before Him in humble adoration and worship. As a matter of fact the boy lay stretched out on the floor in the middle of the room surrounded by the other boys, who listened intently to the message that came through him from the Lord. The boy sobbed and wept with the deepest grief as the message was given to him; he spoke in a clear strong voice, speaking a sentence or two at a time. There was a strong rhythm in the language; the words were simple and pure. The intonation of the voice, the choice of language, the penetrating power of every word was such that no one who heard it could have doubted that this Samuel was speaking by direct supernatural inspiration from God.

In his vision lying at the feet of the Lord the boy said, 'Lord Jesus, I am not worthy to be here or to be saved at all. I am only a little street beggar.' Then Jesus spoke to the boy. The boy did not know it at the time, but the Lord actually used him as a mouthpiece, using the first person and addressing us and the children sitting around him. Our longing is that this message might grip your hearts as it still grips ours.

Christ's message

'I weep tonight. I am heartbroken. I am in deep sorrow because there are so few people who believe in me. I planned and prepared heaven for everyone, and made room for all the people in the world. I made the New Jerusalem in three enormous cities, one above the other, with plenty of space for all. But they will not believe me. Those who believe are so very few. I am sad, so very sad. [This message was given between heart-rending sobs and floods of tears from the boy.] Since men and women will not believe me, I must destroy this wicked earth. I planned to destroy it with three great disasters, but because there is so much evil I have added a fourth.

'If you have any friends, tell them to repent quickly. Persuade everyone to believe the gospel as soon as possible.

But if people will not listen and will not accept your message the responsibility will not be on you.

'Receive the baptism in the Holy Spirit. If you will wait and believe, I will baptize you. The devil deceives you by making you think you will not receive the baptism, but wait and seek, and I will baptize you and give you power to cast out demons and to heal the sick. Those who receive the anointing of the Holy Spirit are to preach and bear witness, and I will be with you to help and protect you in times of danger.

'If you think perhaps you won't get to heaven, that thought is from the devil. I will not destroy my own children; I will protect and save every one of you: not one who belongs to me will be lost. I will overcome. Pray for Mr and Mrs Baker, and I will give them power to cast out demons and to heal the sick. The children in the Home should be obedient. Do not fight. Do not lie. Live at peace. When you pray, pray from your heart. Do not let your love grow cold.

'Tell other churches they too should seek the Holy Spirit. All churches must press forward.

'The devil is coming to the earth in a few years, and there will be great trouble. Do not worry; I will protect you.

'People everywhere will gather together and fight in one place, after which I will come to punish the earth. Do not be afraid, for those who believe in me will be caught up in heaven to blow trumpets and to play harps.

'I will destroy two out of every three people. When I come everything must obey my voice [Chinese: *Yang yang du yao ting o dy hwa*]. Houses will collapse; mountains will fall down; trees will be destroyed. There will be utter destruction and not even a blade of grass will be left [Chinese: *Ih gen tsao du buh liu*]. Those who worship idols will die. All sorcerers and spiritist mediums will be thrown into hell. Only those who believe the gospel will be saved.'

This is what the Lord said to us at Adullam, and we believe this message is for all to whom we may be able to pass it on. It was given in Chinese, as recorded above. The sentences were spoken slowly and distinctly, with pauses in between. I wrote them down as they were given. They were often repeated so that there could be no mistake on the part of the hearers; there was ample time to record every word the Lord spoke through his chosen prophet.

When the message was complete the boy got up and told us he had been at Jesus' feet. He did not know that the Lord had spoken through him in the first person as well as to him. He repeated the prophecy, saying, 'Jesus said this ... Jesus said that.'

Having heard the prophecy, written it down and then heard it repeated from the prophet's memory point by point, it was easy to see how, in the Old Testament days, a scribe could record every word as it came from the prophet's lips or how the prophet himself could record his own messages, saying truly, 'Thus says the Lord'.

Just as in the past God used a boy, Samuel, to speak in an audible voice a message that was directly from God and was fulfilled to the very letter, so we believe that He is still the same living God and has spoken to us directly. We believe this prophecy will be fulfilled. We must either listen and obey, or suffer the eternal consequences.

Chapter 10

The Inspired Word of God

For Christ and His apostles the fact that prophecy was fulfilled proved that the Bible was the inspired Word of God. As we experienced the Holy Spirit move in power at Adullam we too became more than ever convinced of this. We saw these ten biblical prophecies regarding the coming of the Holy Spirit being fulfilled in the lives of the children:

- believers would be baptized in the Holy Spirit;
- they would speak in languages they did not know;
- they would prophesy under the direction of the Holy Spirit;
- they would be given revelations about 'the things of God';
- they would know 'the things to come';
- they would be born again by the Holy Spirit and know that they were children of God;
- *'young men shall see visions'*;[1]
- demons would be cast out;
- the sick would be miraculously healed;
- hearts would be changed so that the children of God loved what once they hated, and hated what once they loved.[2]

God's ways

Since *'God chose the foolish things of the world to shame the wise'* (1 Corinthians 1:27) we should remember that God did not use people with natural ability or education to write the Bible. An uneducated Amos or Peter or John, inspired by God, was able to write more profoundly than the wisest people of this world.

God is still using simple uneducated people today, and the fact that He chose to reveal Himself to the children at Adullam is, for me, another proof of the validity of the Word of God. Jesus still says,

> *'I praise you, Father, Lord of heaven and earth, because you have hidden these things from the wise and learned, and revealed them to little children. Yes, Father, for this was your good pleasure.'* (Matthew 11:25)

These Chinese children did not **learn** these wonderfully profound revelations but they received them through their open hearts, to corroborate what has already been written in the Word of God.

Eye witnesses of past biblical events

The Holy Spirit showed us how Bible writers may have gained an eyewitness knowledge of events which had happened some time in the past. One of our boys who was naturally slow and not very able was on more than one occasion an eyewitness 'in the Spirit' to some of the main historical events of both the Old and New Testaments. He saw the plagues in Egypt: the frogs in Pharaoh's palace, the flies in his food, the locusts, the eldest son dead with the whole family in mourning. He also saw Elijah and Elisha cross the Jordan, the chariots of fire, and Elijah being taken up to heaven, as well as Daniel in the lions' den being protected by angels and other Old Testament events.

He was also given visions of the miracles of Christ. He saw

the temptations of the Lord, with the devil in the form of a handsome young man leading Jesus to a high mountain and in vision showing Him the kingdoms of the world. He was shown angels following Jesus wherever He went, as well as visions of Christ walking on the water, healing the sick and giving sight to the blind. Along with some others this boy also saw the passion of the Lord Jesus, His resurrection and His ascension.

At first I wondered about these visions of past events. I then remembered that with God there is no past, present and future. He is the great 'I AM'. Since the Holy Spirit is His Spirit, through visions and other revelations, the past, present and future may, in God's economy, be made 'present' to any individual the Lord chooses.

These revelations of the past to us at Adullam corroborate the inspiration of the Bible. It was easy for God to take Moses and others in visions through events in the past or in the future as eyewitnesses, and for them to be able to record the past.

Recording revelations from God

The Holy Spirit showed us how some parts of the Bible were written down. When the children were 'in the Spirit' describing scenes they were seeing, the Spirit caused one boy, who was also in a trance, to sit down and go through the motions of writing item by item what the others were seeing and describing. In that way we saw how easy it was for God to write the Bible. One person could record what another saw and described.

If God could do this with simple uneducated children from the streets of China or remote mountain tribes, it must have been just as easy for him to do it with a Barak or any other person of His choosing.

The fact that men and women in the past were moved by the Holy Spirit and prophesied, and were given visions as Isaiah was 'in the year that King Uzziah died', must mean that they can still do so today. They can still be caught up in the Spirit and see the unseen worlds beyond the veil. The same God is still on the throne, reigning over the same world, dealing with the same kind of evil hearts, through the same sort of people, with the same kind of dispositions and passions that Elijah had.

In our own stubborn and unbelieving generation the Lord can and will prove that what He has written in the Bible is the Word of the living God. Among those who believe in Him He can and does move in supernatural ways through gifts of the Holy Spirit, confirming the word with signs following (Mark 16:15–20).

Notes

1. Acts 2:17.
2. Chapter 3 gives more details about how these prophecies were fulfilled, including relevant biblical references.

If you have enjoyed this book and would like to help us to send a copy of it and many other titles to needy pastors in the **Third World**, please write for further information or send your gift to:

Sovereign World Trust
PO Box 777, Tonbridge
Kent TN11 0ZS
United Kingdom

or to the **'Sovereign World'** distributor in your country.

Visit our website at **www.sovereign-world.org** for a full range of Sovereign World books.